Financing Vocational Training in Sub-Saharan Africa

Financing Vocational Training in Sub-Saharan Africa

Adrian Ziderman

THE WORLD BANK
Washington, D.C.

1818 H Street, N.W.
Washington, D.C. 20433
Telephone 202-473-1000
Internet www.worldbank.org
E-mail feedback@worldbank.org

1 2 3 4 05 04 03

Adrian Ziderman, formerly a senior economist at the World Bank, is Professor of Economics at Bar-Ilan University, Israel, and a frequent adviser to international organizations and governments on the evaluation and financing of education and training.

Cover: Instructor Peter A. Makundi teaches diesel fuel injection at the VETA Regional Vocational Training and Service Center in Moshi, Tanzania. Photograph by Richard K. Johanson, World Bank.

ISBN 0-8213-5461-2

Library of Congress Cataloging-in-Publication data has been applied for.

Contents

Tables

Figures

Acknowledgments

This paper was prepared by Adrian Ziderman, Professor of Economics at Bar-Ilan University, Israel. Many individuals and institutions have contributed, directly or indirectly, to its preparation. The author acknowledges the help given, in conversation and through their writings, by the following individuals (listed alphabetically): Amit Dar, Lindsay Falkov, Jutta Franz, Ewald Gold, Richard Johanson, Jon Lauglo, Paud Murphy, Thyra Riley, and Daniel Viens. Amit Dar and Ewald Gold also provided helpful comments on the draft version of the paper (June 2001). Richard Johanson combed through the draft and revised versions of the paper and offered numerous suggestions for improvement, both in substance and presentation. Very helpful feedback on an early version of the paper was received from participants at the seminar on Development of Post-Primary Education in Africa, held at the Institute of Development Studies, University of Sussex in the summer of 2001. Amir Ben-David's professional hand produced the figures.

The Norwegian Education Trust Fund for Africa has generously financed the present study and is, along with the Department for International Development and the World Bank itself, financing the ongoing regional study of vocational skills development. This support is gratefully acknowledged.

Any questions or comments about this report may be addressed to Adrian Ziderman, Economics Department, Bar-Ilan University, Ramat Gan 52900, Israel; email: zidera@mail.biu.ac.il.

Foreword

Skills development is increasingly important in the drive to enhance productivity, stimulate economic competitiveness, and bring people out of poverty. Traditional sources for financing skills development—mainly government budgets—are constrained by economic decline, structural adjustment, and other competing development priorities. New sources of financing are needed to diversify and solidify the base of support for skills development. In addition, financing mechanisms themselves can be used to influence the effectiveness and efficiency of skill development systems.

Professor Adrian Ziderman, one of the authors of the World Bank's work in this field in the early 1990s,* was commissioned to prepare this analysis of training finance. The study first describes the emerging consensus about training finance largely on the basis of experiences in Latin America and Asia. The paper tests this consensus against findings from Sub-Saharan Africa. It then sets out the theoretical basis for different financing mechanisms, including the rationale for state intervention in training markets. The study explores the effects of various types of training levies, different forms of training funds, and the implications of various transfer mechanisms. It also examines the difficult area of financing informal sector training.

* *Vocational and Technical Education and Training: A World Bank Policy Paper*. 1991. Washington, D.C.: The World Bank; Middleton, John, Adrian Ziderman, and Arvil Van Adams. 1993. *Skills for Productivity: Vocational Education and Training in Developing Countries*. New York: Oxford University Press.

The study brings together and synthesizes hitherto inaccessible material on training finance, which was scattered in project documents and unpublished case studies. It includes detailed field investigations of new experiences in South Africa and Tanzania and throws new light on established practice in Zimbabwe and Kenya. The study also emphasizes the wider role of sound funding mechanisms (beyond finance) in leading to effective, demand-oriented training systems. Finally, the study emphasizes policy applications, with detailed discussions of strengths and weaknesses of alternative policies and measures.

This study on training finance forms part of an ongoing regional review of Skills Development in Sub-Saharan Africa. The review is being conducted by the Africa Region of the World Bank and its Human Development Department under the supervision of Richard Johanson and general direction of Arvil Van Adams.

Birger J. Fredriksen
Senior Education Adviser
Africa Region, The World Bank

Preface

The World Bank is undertaking a comprehensive study of postbasic education and training in Sub-Saharan Africa (SSA). This project reviews performance of the lending portfolio, explores individual country studies, highlights and assesses sector issues, and draws together international and regional experience that will be a base for dialogue between the World Bank and its clients. This study is part of that overall review.

By analyzing training financing methods and institutions in SSA countries, this paper derives policy messages for better practices. The paper proceeds logically from theoretical and conceptual issues in the early chapters to more applied treatment of major financing mechanisms in the later ones. Each chapter is meant to be self-standing and may be read independently; however, this inevitably has resulted in some repetition of material across chapters.

In preparation for this paper, three short field studies were conducted in South Africa, Tanzania, and Zimbabwe in early 2001; the findings of these visits, and lessons learned, are reported at relevant points throughout the paper. Because of the detailed nature of the material, of which references to case studies and individual country practice are an integral part, we have also prepared summary tables that present much of the information and findings. And the practical chapters (Chapters 5 through 10) conclude with policy-oriented summary sections that provide some practical advice for policy, including what measures work well, advantages and weaknesses of policy alternatives, and pitfalls to avoid in implementation. Chapter 11 deals with the interplay between national training policy objectives and the main mechanisms for training finance. The final chapter consolidates the paper's main policy messages.

Adrian Ziderman
September 2002

Abbreviations

CINTERFOR	Inter-American Centre for Research and Information on Training
CNFTP	National Council for Technical and Vocational Training (Madagascar)
CVT	Continuing Vocational Training tax (Côte d'Ivoire)
DIT	Directorate of Industrial Training (Kenya)
DTEVT	Department of Technical Education and Vocational Training (Zambia)
FDFP	Vocational Training Development Fund (Côte d'Ivoire)
GTZ	German Agency for Technical Assistance
ILO	International Labour Office
ITB	Industrial training board
INTEP	Integrated Training for Entrepreneurship Promotion (Tanzania)
IVTB	Industrial and Vocational Training Board (Mauritius)
MoHET	Ministry of Higher Education and Technology (Zimbabwe)
MSTVT	Ministry of Science, Technology and Vocational Training (Zambia)
MVTTC	Morogoro Vocational Teachers Training College (Tanzania)
NACVET	National Coordinating Committee for Technical and Vocational Education and Training (Ghana)

NGO	Nongovernmental organization
NVTD	National Vocational Training Division (Tanzania)
NRF	National Revenue Fund (South Africa)
NSSF	National Social Security Fund (Tanzania)
NSA	National Skills Authority (South Africa)
NTA	National training authority
PCO	Project coordination office
RVTSC	Regional Vocational Training and Service Center (Tanzania)
SARS	South African Revenue Service
SETA	Sector Education and Training Authority (South Africa)
SSA	Sub-Saharan Africa
TAP	Traditional Apprenticeship Programme (Zimbabwe)
TEVETA	Technical Education, Vocational and Entrepreneurship Training Authority (Zambia)
TRA	Tax Revenue Authority (Tanzania)
VET	Vocational education and training
VETA	Vocational Education and Training Authority (Tanzania)
VTC	Vocation training center
ZIMDEF	Zimbabwe Manpower Development Fund

Executive Summary

To meet the skills needs of economies, societies, and individuals, national training systems must be:

- *Effective:* offering meaningful, quality skills development that avoids time-serving and irrelevant training
- *Efficient:* avoiding high costs and inefficient provision
- *Competitive:* to counter supply-driven training tendencies
- *Flexible:* technically able in the short term to change the scope and direction of training outputs, if necessary
- *Responsive:* designed to meet the changing demands of the market and needs of the economy.

A central theme of this paper is that training finance mechanisms, in addition to supplying funding for the national training system, play a central role in achieving these overall policy objectives.

Challenges to conventional patterns of financing training

Traditionally, the financial burden of training has fallen, alone or in concert, on trainees, enterprises, and the state.

As in the past, the vast majority of employment across SSA countries today is within small-scale, informal sector enterprises. Initial training for the informal sector took place on the job, through the traditional, unstructured apprenticeship, with trainees (or their families) bearing the costs of training in the form of an initial lump-sum payment and/or a low (apprentice) wage.

Formal sector training shows a different financing pattern. Where enterprise training provides general, transferable skills, the trainee-apprentice bears the implicit cost of training through low wages. To the extent that training is not transferable, the enterprise assumes some of the financial burden of initial training. Training in preemployment skills acquired in private markets at proprietary training institutions is paid for by students.

These forms of training take place within private markets and are essentially demand-driven, focused on meeting market demands for skills.

Nearly all SSA countries have established public training systems; they constitute the leading supplier of structured, preemployment training, frequently dominating the market as providers of formal sector training. But the state is also a major financier of preemployment training; public training institutions provide courses free or at purely nominal fees.

This simple financing framework, still current in many SSA countries, can no longer meet society's skill development needs. A number of emerging trends have rendered this framework obsolete:

- Many training systems have a tendency to market failure, with firms undertraining in transferable skills, both in the amount and quality of training. The consequent shortages of well-trained, skilled workers in the formal sector stunts productivity, competitiveness, and industrial development.

- Technological change, structural adjustment policies, new and changing patterns of trade and competition, and globalization have compelled the need for a much more flexible and responsive training system for the modern sector than past regimes have allowed.

- Fiscal restraint is central in structural adjustment policies. Limited public sector budgets have seriously constrained the ability of SSA governments to provide stable funding to the public training sector. In other

SSA economies, a heavy reliance on indirect taxes for revenues has spawned tight public budgets, and broadening the tax base may not be feasible.

- In many SSA countries, demographic change and high population growth rates have substantially increased the numbers entering the labor force. The result has been high unemployment, underemployment, and low wages, especially for young people. Since the formal employment sector remains small and stagnant with little growth potential, an expanding urban informal sector is becoming a major source of manpower absorption and employment growth.
- There is a growing social awareness (and conscience) about the needs of special groups, such as the poor, ethnic minorities, and women. There is also a wider acceptance that the government has an obligation to assist through financing and perhaps skills provision; these developments are likely being held back by a lack of government funding, indicating an appropriate role for donor intervention.

SSA training systems, and the ways in which they are financed, will have to adapt to the new realities. This adaptation will require a reexamination of the current role of the state, enterprises, and individuals in training markets and how these roles will need to change. Change will include the development of private training markets, increased competition between public and private training providers, declining roles for the state in the financing and provision of training, a greater diversification of funding sources for skills development (including enhanced cost recovery, cost sharing, and training taxes), encouragement of more and higher-quality enterprise training, and meeting the special needs of the informal sector.

Redefined government role

Funding mechanisms are aimed in part at augmenting training resources. In conventional training markets, the state, rather than the direct beneficiaries, bears most of the financial burden of formal sector training, particularly preemployment training. Government has reached out to new sources of financing (either to fund or expand the current training system). But apart from the cost burden, is government funding of training excessive in relation to funding needs? Against the background provided by a closer look at the factors justifying government financing of training, the appropriate role for governmental intervention in financial training markets may be more readily discussed.

Seven arguments may be offered to justify government's role in financing and providing training:

- Externalities
- Property rights in human capital within the enterprise
- Market imperfections
- Inadequate enterprise training
- Weak private training institutional capacity
- Parity of treatment between trainees and students
- Neglect of disadvantaged groups.

The first five arguments lead to undersupply of trained workers; the last two, social arguments, focus on inequities and the neglect of the economically weak.

None of these arguments (except to supplement weak, private training institutional capacity) makes a case for the state to provide training. The case for public subsidy of training is strongest where there are external effects of training and in support of skill development for disadvantaged groups. The role of government in both financing and providing training is probably excessive in many SSA countries.

While there is usually much more public *provision* of training than required by economic rationale alone, this may be justified if public training is efficient, effective, and market-responsive. Unfortunately, this is usually not the case. And, again, there is far more public *financing* of training than can be justified by the economic arguments alone.

The appropriate role of government in training markets cannot be determined without knowing the capabilities of private training markets. Where they function well, private training markets can be an alternative to the public sector; where they do not then the public sector should be engaged. This approach requires that a country determine its individual needs for intervention in public sector training. It will have to examine the performance of its training markets, the capacity of the private sector to deliver training, and its own preferences about social policies and equity. On this basis, the state is likely to retain a central role in the delivery and, particularly, financing of training in most SSA countries.

National training funds

Some 30 SSA countries have established training funds. A national training fund is a unique institutional framework for unifying and augmenting public sources of funding, as well as for allocating funds in line with national policies and priorities. In older, established training funds, training levies were the dominant (usually only) income source; newer funds draw from a variety of income sources, including government allocations, donor funding, and income generated by the fund itself. Indeed, in some cases training funds derive no income from training levies; either levies have not been instituted or, where in place, levy proceeds are regarded as general tax revenues and not passed on to the fund.

Earlier training funds based on payroll levies were largely single purpose—that is, either aimed at financing public sector preemployment training (revenue-generating schemes), or at enhancing the amount and quality of enterprise training investment (levy-grant schemes). Some funds had mixed objectives. But in all cases, levy income was not only committed to predesignated disbursement targets, but there was also a large degree of consonance between those financing the levy and those receiving the training benefits.

With the broadening of training funds, both in terms of sources and disbursements, this link has been considerably weakened. Training funds are now increasingly seen as a general funding pool, distributed across various recipient destinations according to established priorities and policies. This situation may result in a considerable degree of cross-subsidization of training (such as informal sector training from formal sector levy proceeds).

Disbursement

There are four main categories for fund disbursement (funding windows). Each one aims at distinct client groups (with some degree of overlap), responding to different training needs and policy objectives.

- Core funding to training institutions for preemployment skills development, aimed largely at formal sector employment. Government support of such training at public training institutions is a central element in conventional training markets; similarly, revenue-raising payroll levy schemes support this training.
- Training incentives offered to enterprises in the formal sector where initial training (including apprenticeship training) or continuing training is deemed insufficient. These incentives may take the form of direct training subsidies to companies or reimbursement of training levies.
- Training courses for the unemployed and other disadvantaged, either through financing special courses at public training institutions or, preferably, by contracting for its provision, following public tender that is open to both public and private training providers.
- Meeting the training needs of microenterprises and the informal sector, where these conventional private markets are inadequate to meet the changing needs of this growing, more technologically based sector.

The range of institutions and forms of training eligible for funding may vary markedly from case to case; they are usually designated in the legislation setting up the fund. In many SSA countries, the precarious state of public budgets, combined with the limited income from payroll levies, will require strict disbursement priorities. The relatively small size of the formal employment sector and its lack of growth, combined with the considerable growth potential for informal sector employment, may indicate the need for a different pattern of disbursement priorities than is found in other regions. In many SSA countries, core finance for preemployment courses at training institutions, together with innovative methods of financing training for microenterprises and the informal sector, should be first in disbursement priorities. Whatever the merits of such expenditures, pressures on public budgets are likely to result in the neglect of disadvantaged groups, unless designated funding is forthcoming from donor sources.

Fund sustainability

National training funds (particularly when financed by company training levies) should provide sustained and stable funding for the training programs they support. This has not always happened, especially when funds do not receive the resources designated for their activities; for example, training levy proceeds meant for the training fund may instead be absorbed into general government revenues. Long-term training fund sustainability is a serious problem in some countries, especially where training funds have been launched by donors and are mainly funded externally. This problem will be endemic in the many SSA countries whose public budgets will be severely constrained in the medium term, and that are not ready to introduce training levies. In these situations, overgenerous external support for national training funds, without the planned development of domestic funding, will result in moribund training authorities and empty coffers.

Training authorities

Where institutionally possible, fully fledged, autonomous national training authorities should be established and charged with the central role of assuming responsibility for national skills development. To respond to the developing skill needs of the economy—and to be proactive in regard to technological and industrial change—public training systems need more independence from line ministries. National training authorities will often play a central coordinating role in planning the national training system, developing training policy, supervising national skills testing and certification, providing information services, and developing appropriate labor market signals.

Conditions for training fund success

Successful outcomes depend on six conditions:

- *Secure income for the fund:* Ensure adequate levels, stability, and sustainability of training fund incomes
- *Fund management autonomy:* Ensure decisionmaking autonomy of the management board and its control over budget allocations

- *Stakeholder ownership:* Substantial representation of the major stakeholders on the management board, engendering a sense of ownership—particularly of employer groups where training levies are in place
- *Restricting fund activities to national training needs:* Ensure that training fund policies and disbursements are targeted according to defined national training needs; avoid extraneous (nontraining) activities
- *Avoid the role of training provider:* Training centers run (and financed) by a training fund tend to receive high subsidies and preferential treatment; this distorts training markets and hinders moves toward an open, competitive training system
- *Transparent decisionmaking:* Decisionmaking is to be open and, in particular, the basis for fund allocation is to be understood.

Training levies

Earmarked levies on enterprise payrolls have become the most widely adopted mechanism for funding training, both in public training institutions (usually under the aegis of a national training fund/authority) and in enterprises. They are central to training-finance policies in many SSA countries, while other countries are now examining the benefits and feasibility of introducing payroll levies to finance training.

The scope for levying payroll taxes is well established by international experience, in SSA, and elsewhere. Almost all the countries that have introduced payroll levies have set a standard national levy rate in the range of 1 to 2 percent of company payroll bills, most at the lower end of the range. Some SSA countries have introduced sector-level training taxes, usually (but not always) based on payrolls. The main advantage is that they offer a means of tailoring the levy format to the specific needs and characteristics of the sector in question. Yet, the narrow focus of sectoral levies (and the training funds they finance) prevents an integrated, national approach to the finance and planning of skills development. This has precluded their broad adoption, and most countries have wisely employed standard, national-level levy schemes, based on enterprise payrolls.

Types of payroll levies

National payroll tax schemes are usually classified into two distinct groups, reflecting different underlying objectives: revenue-generation schemes (where levy proceeds finance training provided by public sector institutions) and levy-grant schemes (aimed at encouraging investment in training by firms themselves). This traditional dichotomy is becoming outdated, however, as evolving levy schemes take on a broader range of tasks, particularly in the context of developing national training funds and training authorities.

Revenue generation. Levy proceeds are used mainly to support public sector training, with the emphasis on initial training at formal public training institutions. In the SSA context especially, this kind of payroll levy scheme can be a mechanism for greater funding diversification, easing the state's burden of funding training. The expectation that levy income would complement existing government financing, thus providing an additional source of funding, has not always happened in practice, with levy income displacing government subventions. There are also notable cases of the opposite tendency, where "earmarked" training taxes are absorbed into general government revenues rather than being used for the financing of public training.

Levy-grant schemes. Levy-grant schemes focus on company in-service training. They create incentives for a firm to invest more in the skills development of its work force, be it on-the-job training (setting up or extending and improving existing company training) or external training for workers. The need for government intervention, via the introduction of levy-grant arrangements, arises because of shortcomings in the amount and/or quality of enterprise training. While there are numerous variants, a threefold classification of levy-grant schemes has been widely adopted: cost reimbursement, cost redistribution, and levy exemption.

- *Cost reimbursement.* The training fund pays grants to firms on a cost-incurred basis for designated kinds of training (both on the job and off the job). The purpose of these schemes is often misunderstood, particularly among employers. The scheme does not intend to reimburse the levy as such, but rather to reimburse incurred training costs (to encourage firms to train more or better). Thus, a training expenditure reimbursement ceiling (for firms that train to acceptable standards) is usually set, up to a given percentage of the levy paid. This is the variant generally adopted in SSA.

- *Cost redistribution.* Designed especially to deal with the ill effects of the poaching of skilled workers by nontraining firms, the scheme redistributes training expenditures toward companies that do train. Training companies may receive grants far in excess of the amount of the levy paid, providing strong incentives for firms to train. There are few examples of cost-redistribution schemes in the SSA region.
- *Levy exemption.* Usually employed as part of broader cost-reimbursement schemes, levy exemption allows firms that are meeting their training needs to withdraw from the levy-grant system, or at least to benefit from reduced levy assessments. A major advantage is that levy exemption frees firms from the bureaucratic fatigues of levy payment and subsequent grant claim; also, potential cash flow problems are avoided. While much discussed, this mechanism is found more often in industrial economies than in developing countries.

Advantages and limitations

If moving toward policy reform, the strengths and advantages of payroll taxes should be set against their possible dangers and limitations. Payroll levies have the following advantages:

- Diversify the revenue base for financing training by mobilizing additional revenues
- Can provide a stable and protected source of funding for national training; this is especially important where budgets are insecure
- When part of a levy-grant system, can encourage firms to intensify their training efforts, increase training capacity, and raise training quality
- A strong case can be made for viewing earmarked payroll levies as "benefit taxation"

- Training levies collected from formal sector employers can be a vehicle for cross- subsidization of training, especially from the formal to the informal sector.

Payroll levies have the following limitations:

- Many firms, particularly small ones, do not benefit from the scheme; this breeds resentment and opposition and compromises the status of training levies as "benefit taxation"
- Earmarked taxation does not conform well with the principles of sound public finance and weakens any attempts to unify the national tax system
- Under fiscal pressure, government may incorporate training levy proceeds into general public tax revenues
- Levy proceeds may be diverted to nontraining uses
- Payroll levies may constitute an oversheltered source of funding, leading to unspent surpluses, inefficiencies, and top-heavy bureaucracies
- Payroll levies raise the cost of labor to the employer, possibly discouraging employment
- Employers may shift the incidence of the levy onto workers in the form of lowered wages; in this case, workers and not the employers bear the burden of the tax.

Issues in levy scheme design and implementation

SSA countries have a lower success rate with training levies than do other regions. Design and implementation of levy schemes will need special attention in order to secure the benefits of payroll levies while avoiding the weaknesses evident within the SSA context. These issues include the following:

- *Levy rate:* Levy rates must be subject by law to periodic review to avoid the accumulation of surpluses
- *National or sectoral levy rates:* A standard, national payroll levy rate (rather than differing sectoral rates) will be appropriate in most SSA countries

- *Sectoral coverage:* Levy coverage should be as wide as possible across economic sectors and include public enterprises
- *Company size:* Very small firms should be exempt from levy payment, on the grounds of both efficiency and equity
- *Levy collection:* Effective agents should have control of levy collection; self-collection by funding organizations should be avoided
- *Security of levy proceeds:* Government must be prevented from raiding levy revenues (especially where tax authorities act as the collection agent) by placing funds in special, closed accounts
- *Employer buy-in:* Employers should be involved in forming and executing payroll levy policy
- *Premature introduction of payroll levies:* Payroll levies may be inappropriate where levy-income-generating capacity is weak—either because of the limited size of the formal sector or administrative difficulties in collecting levies.

Finance mechanisms: augmenting funding for training

Virtually all the training systems in SSA have to deal with the reality of diminishing government funding for public sector training, partly because of the structural adjustment policies and increasing demands on government funding by competing sectors. The response is greater funding diversification—seeking alternative or additional funding for public training from other sources.

Four different ways to diversify funding can be pursued separately or in combination:

- *Fund augmentation.* Public sector training funds available for supporting training institutions via subventions may be augmented from other sources. The classic method is to impose special taxes, earmarked for training.
- *Cost sharing.* Training costs may be shared with the beneficiaries of training, mainly by introducing training course fees or by raising them

to levels that are more realistic. These measures will allow a reduction in public subsidies for training.

- *Income generation.* Training institutions may seek income from other sources, such as by selling products (combining production with training) or renting out facilities.
- *Private training provision.* Developing private training institutions may be encouraged, thus generating additional funding for training and, in parallel, reducing the call on public funds. This approach is especially relevant where expanding the training system is desirable.

The first three approaches bring additional revenues directly into the training sector, while the fourth affects training budgets only indirectly. Of the direct funding methods, the first increases the size of the funding available for distribution to training institutions, but there is no immediate effect on the income of individual training institutions. Diversification options are not alternatives; all four avenues can be explored simultaneously. Whether or not to do so and to what extent, however, remains a policy issue that must be settled within the context of country conditions.

Fund augmentation

Earmarked training taxes, levied on the payrolls of enterprises, have become the most widely adopted alternative to central government budgetary allocations. Training levies can be a stable and protected source of funding for national training provision; in many cases, the declared intention of a payroll levy is to lighten public sector financing burdens. There remains the danger, however, that because of funding pressures from other government activities, this process may be taken too far, with levy income replacing rather than complementing government funding.

Cost sharing

Unlike fund augmentation, which results in a larger funding pool, cost sharing intends to reduce the size of allocations to individual training institutions. The best known and most widely used method is to impose or raise the level of user fees to trainees or students enrolled in training courses.

There is little conformity in tuition fees policy across SSA countries. The feasibility of tuition fee setting (in relation to unit costs of training) is a compound of many and diverse factors that vary from place to place. They include (a) type and costs of training, (b) the price elasticity of trainee demand for training courses, (c) political constraints, and (d) policies for equal opportunity. Thus, the scope for generating revenues from tuition fees will have to be settled on a case-by-case basis, in the light of local conditions.

Fee policies will have to determine whether a regime of standard, national compulsory fees should be instituted, or whether individual training institutions should be free to fix the level of fees overall, differing by the type of training course. Institutional autonomy is more desirable because it will encourage training providers to develop a more dynamic, even aggressive, approach to exploiting the potential of the local market environment. This is how institutional fee policy becomes more than a device for cost recovery and cost sharing—that is, in providing a mechanism for different fee levels across courses and client groups, it serves as a tool for moving toward a more open, demand-driven training system. The voluntary setting of user fees, however, may not be feasible in otherwise centralized training systems. While standard, compulsory fee setting may be an inflexible tool, unlikely to reflect local market realities, it is generally acceptable as a second-best measure for reducing pressures on public budgets.

The positive financial benefits from greater cost recovery need to be examined alongside the potentially adverse effects on equity. There is a clear tradeoff here. Higher, realistic fees will exclude those unable to pay for training; fees set at comfortably low levels will not help cost recovery. In particular, access to training will be more difficult for the poor, minorities, rural populations, and other disadvantaged groups. This situation points to the need for targeted subsidies directed to these at-risk groups, in the form of scholarships and reduced fees. However, targeting those *most* in need within these groups, particularly in the SSA context, has not been easy.

Cost sharing through user fees will discourage participation in formal training programs, even by the nonpoor. The classic solution to this problem, encountered most frequently in higher education, is deferred cost recovery in the form of student loan schemes. But the track record of student loan schemes in SSA is poor. The sound administration of a loan scheme requires appropriate, high-level, institutional support, which is at a premium in many SSA countries. Given the lack of success in administering student loan schemes in SSA, it is not likely that training loans would fare better.

Institutional income generation

Revenue from the sale of production and service activities of trainees can augment institutional income. Income may be derived as a byproduct of the training process itself. But it is also possible to use available skills and facilities to produce output for sale in the local market. Indeed, exposure to local markets may lead to market-oriented training. The issue is one of maintaining a healthy balance between these two activities. As more weight is given to instruction, the income potential from production declines; alternatively, training quality will suffer as production is emphasized over instruction.

The proportion of recurrent expenses covered by production sales will vary considerably, depending on numerous local factors, including the nature of the product, local demand conditions, and potential market competition. If a balance is maintained between training quality and production for sale, the scope for cost recovery may be limited, usually accounting for only a small percentage of recurrent expenditure. In some exceptional cases, however, it can contribute a considerable proportion of total costs.

Training institutions may also generate income from selling services, including renting out underused facilities and providing consulting services to local enterprises.

As with training fee policy, local institutional initiative in generating income from production will be stunted if this income does not contribute to institutional budgets. This is the case where the sums collected are deducted from institutional budgetary allocations and thus accrue to government budgets or the national training fund, and not to the training institution. Institutional fee charging and income-generation objectives can be enhanced through decentralized control over public sector providers and greater institutional autonomy. It is only then that the full potential of cost sharing and income generation will be achieved.

Encouraging private provision

The growth of private training institutions, with trainees paying full costs, is a way to expand the national training system without heavy commitments of public funds. Indeed, reduced public training provision could be possible (and concomitant budgetary reductions), with the reduction in public training supply made up for by a compensating expansion of private training institutions.

In many SSA countries, the lack of private training results from constraints on the development of private training institutions, including financial constraints, issues of fee policy, regulation and control of private institutions, and information gaps.

- *Financial constraints.* A lack of capital resources, combined with financial market imperfections, may seriously hinder the development of these incipient training institutions, especially for high-cost industrial and technical courses. To offset limited capital market access, governments may offer development loans or subsidies, particularly in strategic skill areas, to assist these firms in their start-up phases. Equipment grants and subsidies for staff development may also be warranted.

- *Fee policy.* Imposed tuition fee ceilings, while aimed at protecting trainees from being exploited by private training institutions, may too rigidly limit the ability of these institutions to enter new training markets, especially those with high investment and recurrent costs.

- *Regulation.* Private training institutions are unlikely to flourish in an overly strict regulatory environment. Regulation and enforcement should be sparing; they should be strong enough to counter dishonest practices and low-quality training, and should encourage private training institutions to operate fairly and efficiently within a facilitating, regulatory environment.

- *Consumer information.* Without reliable information, consumers are unable to make wise choices, and information on both the quality and stability of private training institutions is often lacking. In addition, the provision of updated information on the relevance of courses to labor market demands and job opportunities is important.

Funding distribution: transfers to training institutions

The allocation among training providers of the total government budget for training is a major component of the financing system in SSA countries. In most cases, there is no clearly formulated, objective disbursement policy. The arbitrary, ad hoc institutional core funding arrangements in place in almost all SSA countries should be dismantled and gradually replaced by objective funding formula, such as those related to inputs, outputs, and outcomes.

These reforms are important because the mechanism through which government transfers funds to training institutions affects the way in which this funding is used, as well as general institutional behavior. Inherent shortcomings in the transfer mechanisms now used promote low internal efficiency and a strengthening of supply-driven training. Funding disbursement policies must provide an appropriate mix of regulation and incentives to ensure that public training can hold its own in an environment of competitive training markets.

Moves toward objective criteria seem well within the grasp of the governments in many SSA countries, and there has been some promising experimentation with these methods in current training institution reform in the region. Barriers to progress stem more from institutional resistance, opposition of vested interests, and the slowness of higher education institutions, which would be expected to lead the way. But change could well be on the horizon in countries formulating a broad package of institutional reform. Objective funding criteria might then become part of a general reform of institutional funding, which would include reduced public funding overall (replaced by cost recovery and income generation), decentralization and enhanced institutional autonomy, and greater use of contact funding.

Encouraging enterprise training

A legitimate response to the tendency of firms to undertrain is to offer incentives that encourage firms to train. These may be provided as:

- Direct subsidy of enterprise training out of public funds
- Training cost reimbursement, as part of a levy-grant system
- Indirectly, through concessions on company tax obligations for firms that train.

Alternative forms of subsidy

Levy-grant systems (where the training grant to the enterprise is financed by a training levy) have some clear advantages over the two alternative incentive systems—direct government subsidy payments and concessions on enterprise tax obligations. A major advantage of levy-grant systems is that they do not draw on public funds, a point of some importance in times of tight government budgets. In addition, they can lead to a more systematic, structured approach to training. Underprovision of training suffers not only from too low levels of training, but also from training that is piecemeal and not integrated.

The response to direct and indirect subsidy schemes may be low because they are not focused enough to catch the attention of senior management. But in the case of levy-grant schemes, "involvement" is ensured by the compulsory payment of the levy; anecdotal evidence suggests that senior company finance officers exert pressure on the training function to ensure that "we get back the levy."

The disadvantages of tax concession schemes have militated against their adoption in other than a very few SSA countries. They require a well-developed and broadly based system of corporate taxation, often lacking in SSA countries, and the number of firms responding may be low because few of them earn enough profits to benefit from tax exemptions.

All three mechanisms share a number of weaknesses. These include:

- *Windfalls.* Eligible training may have been provided by the enterprise even in the absence of the incentive scheme.
- *Training distortions* may bias training toward more formal and externally provided training, away from informal training on the job.

- *Repackaging* may lead to the adaptation and documentation of existing training provisions to comply with eligibility requirements.
- *Inspection costs.* The central costs of inspection and monitoring, to counter abuse by enterprises, may be high.
- *Administrative burden.* The cost to the enterprise of establishing eligibility and compliance (including paperwork and record-keeping) may be high. A central problem in training grant design is to minimize the effects of these weaknesses.

Subsidizing apprentice wages

In many SSA countries, apprenticeship training is a key method of skills development for the formal employment sector. Support for apprenticeship training, in the form of subsidizing the wages of apprentices, is often part of a wider regime of government training subsidies or levy-grant schemes, as described above. A particular case can be made for subsidized apprenticeship wages on both equity and efficiency grounds.

Apprentice wage subsidies can be a useful tool, positively influencing the quantity of initial training that companies provide; however, some preconditions must be present:

- Employers cannot exploit the availability of apprentice wage subsidies to gain access to cheap labor.
- The elasticity of supply of apprenticeship slots is not low; otherwise, the desired supply response of an increased apprenticeship intake will not occur.
- On-the-job apprenticeship training must provide genuine training and skills development for the worker, in turn imposing costs on the firm that are offset (in part or full) by the wage subsidy.

Needs of disadvantaged groups

Any package to assist disadvantaged groups should include a continuing and enhanced government role in skills development. There is a growing social awareness (and conscience) about the low status and skill needs of special groups, such as the poor, ethnic minorities, and women. There is also a wide recognition that the government has an obligation to assist in this field, through financing and perhaps through provision of special programs, aimed particularly at securing entry into the informal sector. However, these developments will face heavy constraints because of increasingly limited public budgets and greater intersectoral competition for funding allocations. This may indicate an appropriate role for donor intervention.

Financing informal sector training

The largely neglected training needs of small microenterprises and informal sector producers must be addressed. Throughout SSA countries, considerable population (and labor force) growth, combined with minimal employment increases in the combined public and formal private sectors, places an increasing absorption burden on the informal sector. While traditional informal sector training markets, characterized by unstructured within-firm skills acquisition, continue to serve the sector well, the system is too narrow to cope with the challenges brought on by technical change, skills enhancement, and the widening of geographical markets. Public institutional training has not been able adapt to the skill needs of the informal sector. Thus, an increasingly central role for specialized training providers (external to the firm) is now seen, both for entry training into new skill areas and developing markets, as well as for informal sector workers and proprietors. Private markets have not been able to fill this void, thus defining a critical role for government initiatives, perhaps buttressed by donor support.

Voucher schemes, though still mostly experimental, are operational in a number of SSA countries. They aim at building up consumer demand for training courses for the informal sector and at facilitating a competitive response among training providers through the exercising of consumer choice of training institution and course offering. Vouchers typically do not lighten the financing burden falling on the funding body; training remains subsidized, and cost recovery is not an integral part of the scheme (though it may be present). But vouchers can lead to greater cost-effectiveness of training provision, wider consumer (trainee) choice, and an improved demand-orientation of training for the informal sector.

Applications to policy

The reader is referred to the final two summary chapters, where, respectively, financing mechanisms are matched with policy objectives, and major policy messages are summarized.

CHAPTER 1

Introduction

A decade ago, the World Bank issued its policy paper on training in developing countries (*Vocational and Technical Education and Training: A World Bank Policy Paper,* May 1991), followed by a detailed account of the research on which it was based (Middleton, Ziderman, and Adams 1993). These publications have been a basis for defining appropriate training policies and projects that lead to better practice in the field—and the finance of training was a central theme in this work. These publications, however, did not address the needs of specific regions or different levels of development.

This paper provides a specific study of training finance needs and policies within the regional context of Sub-Saharan African (SSA). While there is a great deal of case material on recent training finance experiences in SSA, it tends to be scattered in project documents and unpublished case studies. This material has never been bought together formally, and there has been little updating of this knowledge base. Little evidence has been gathered to access systematically the effectiveness of funding innovations in the 1990s. One exception is analytical work carried out by the World Bank and the International Labour Office (ILO) on vocational education and training in the second half of the 1990s, which included three case studies on reforms in SSA countries, (Gill, Dar, and Fluitman 2000). Coverage of financing issues in these case studies, however, was scant.

Training finance: consensus from the literature

Over the last decade, a number of overviews of issues linked to training finance in developing countries have appeared. These overviews have focused on both theoretical issues and practice. Major contributions to this literature include: Inter-American Centre for Research and Information on Training [CINTERFOR]/ILO (1990),[1] Ziderman (1990),[2] Dougherty and Tan (1991),[3] Ducci (1991), Herschbach (1993), Gasskov (1994), Wallenborn (1994), Bolina (1994), Atchoarena (1996), Gill, Dar, and Fluitman (2000), and Jager and Buhrer (2000). While a few dissenting voices have arisen,[4] this literature is notable for the large measure of unity in general approach and conformity in the findings and recommendations of the constituent contributors. In this section we draw together some of the central elements of this "emerging consensus" and pose the question: What may be derived from this literature for a better understanding of training finance practice and reform in SSA?

The main elements of this consensus may be summarized as follows: Central to all is the policy objective of developing an effective, efficient, competitive, flexible, and responsive training system. This system will be demand-driven—that is, training provision that aims at meeting the skill needs of the economy, of society, and of individuals.

Each of the five elements is critical for success. Training systems should be (a) *effective:* offer meaningful, quality skills development, avoiding time-serving and irrelevant training; (b) *efficient:* avoid high-cost, inefficient provision; (c) *competitive:* to counter supply-driven training tendencies and facilitate the development of training effectiveness and efficiency; (d) *flexible:* technically able in the short term to change the scope and direction of outputs (training provision) if necessary; and (e) *responsive:* designed to be responsive to the changing demands of the market and the economy.

Financing mechanisms have a central role to play in achieving this overall policy objective. In particular, a reconsideration of government's dominant role in the financing and provision of training at public training institutions will be required. A redefined (and diminished, but still critical) government role will entail reduced public budgetary support for formal sector training, accompanied by a diversification of sources of financing, greater cost recovery, and cost sharing. Public funding of training institutions would move away from arbitrary, ad hoc funding arrangements to objective formula funding related to inputs, outputs, and outcomes.

Moves toward increased cost sharing will mean the imposition of higher, more realistic training fees accompanied by scholarships for disadvantaged groups and perhaps state-backed student loan schemes. More voice would be given to trainee/consumer choice; voucher schemes may provide a mechanism for developing the demand side of the market in those situations where subsidy needs to be retained, at least over the short term.

Funding diversification measures include training levies on enterprises and enhanced income generation by public training institutions. Government should encourage and facilitate the growth of private sector provision where feasible. This encouragement will provide a desirable, competitive framework for the formal training sector as a whole, leading to more effective, open, and cost-effective provision. Government institutional funding should address the need to offer incentives for efficient, market-oriented training, using such devices as output funding and contract training. Funding allocations would be made on a competitive basis, with the aim of raising institutional efficiency, integrating training markets, and moving toward demand-driven provision. These objectives would be supported through parallel policies for decentralized control over public sector providers and greater institutional autonomy.

Where formal sector enterprises undertrain, levy-grant mechanisms may be useful in encouraging firms to increase investments in developing the skills of their workers. The development of national training funds is an encouraging trend, indicating recognition that training expenditures must be viewed in a long-term, national context. Where institutionally possible, fully fledged, autonomous national training authorities should be established (or the responsibilities of training funds broadened), charged with forming and guiding national training policy. Participation of the main stakeholders (especially employers) is important in national training policy formation and management. This participation may be achieved, for example, by providing an active, participatory role for major stakeholders in the governance of national training funds and training authorities. Participation has an important role to play in building national consensus on training issues, which may be especially important where training levies are imposed on enterprises.

Attention also would be given to the particular, and largely neglected, training needs of small microenterprises and informal sector producers. Finally, there should be a continuing and enhanced government role in skills development as part of a package to assist disadvantaged groups.

The 15 central elements of the emerging policy consensus are summarized in Table 1.1.

Approach and methodology

In terms of this paper's focus on SSA experience, the available literature is limited in a number of ways. While these reviews often contain good, detailed discussions of individual innovative financing mechanisms, they lack a broad contextual framework and, in particular, a clear discussion of how the various measures relate to each other and to the training finance system as a whole. Many contributions discuss different financing mechanisms within defined categories. Thus, Herschbach (1993) classifies training finance mechanisms largely in terms of the sources of the funding (through public revenue, enterprise financing, fees, and so on), an approach closely followed by Bolina (1994). The report from KODIS Consult GmbH (Jager and Buhrer 2000) categorizes and discusses financing mechanisms in terms of whether training is financed unilaterally (that is, exclusively by one of the stakeholders, be it the state, employers, or trainees) or is cofinanced. Dougherty and Tan (1991, 1997) discuss financing according to use (subsidies and other incentives) and sources of finance.

This paper takes a different approach. Initially, we emphasize the viewing of individual financing mechanisms within the context of the system of training finance flows as a whole. In particular, we focus on the differing objectives of these mechanisms. Thus, it seems important to distinguish among (a) mechanisms primarily aimed at broadening the sources of funding (funding diversification); (b) those mainly concerned with improving the allocation and effective use of funding by training providers; (c) mechanisms aimed at offering incentives for more and better training, particularly enterprise-based training; and (d) mechanisms designed to improve the overall efficiency of training markets. Since training finance mechanisms ultimately help achieve defined policy objectives, toward the end of the paper we categorize mechanisms in terms of the policy objectives they are designed to advance. This categorization may guide discussions about the efficacy of different mechanisms for meeting these objectives.

Table 1.1 Training Finance: The Emerging Policy Consensus

Overall training policy objective:
To facilitate the development of effective, efficient, competitive, flexible and responsive (demand-driven) training markets, to meet national economic and social needs and the needs of individuals

Role of training finance in moving towards this objective	Explanation	Detailed discussion in chapter
Redefined government role	Redefinition of government role (diminished, but still critical), entailing reduced public budgetary support for formal sector institutional training	3
Funding diversification	Diminished state financing is to be accompanied by diversification of sources of funding, greater cost recovery and cost sharing	7
Cost sharing	Moves towards increased cost sharing, with higher, more realistic training fees (with scholarships for the needy) and perhaps state-backed student/trainee loans	7
Training levies	Funding diversification measures to include training levies on enterprises	6 and 7
Income generation	Funding diversification measures also include income generation by public training institutions	7
Decentralization	Income generation objectives would be furthered through decentralization of control over public sector providers and greater institutional autonomy	7
Private sector	Government to encourage private sector provision of training	7
Funding public training institutions	Replace arbitrary, ad hoc funding arrangements by objective formula funding related to inputs, outputs, and outcomes. Consider case for subsidy of selected private training institutions	8
Trainee/consumer choice	More voice is to be accorded to trainee/consumer choice; vouchers may help develop the demand side of the market where subsidy needs to be retained	8
Levy-grant systems	Levy-grant mechanisms to be introduced where formal sector enterprises undertrain	6 and 9
Training funds	National training funds to be developed, to take a broader and longer-term view of training expenditures in a national context	5
Training authorities	Where institutionally possible, fully fledged, autonomous national training authorities to be established	5

(Continued)

Table 1.1 *(continued)*

Overall training policy objective: To facilitate the development of effective, efficient, competitive, flexible and responsive (demand-driven) training markets, to meet national economic and social needs and the needs of individuals		
Role of training finance in moving towards this objective	Explanation	Detailed discussion in chapter
Stakeholders	Increased participation of stakeholders (especially employers) in national training policy formation and execution	5
Disadvantaged groups	Continuing and enhanced government role in skills development as an integral part of measures to assist disadvantaged groups	10
Informal sector	Central attention to be paid to largely neglected training needs of small and micro enterprises and informal sector producers	10

Much of the literature is developed in general, rather than country-specific, terms. To the extent that it does draw on practical examples and detailed case studies, these are limited in number and largely drawn from experience outside SSA countries. Thus, in their discussion on the international experience with training incentives, Dougherty and Tan (1991) provide sections on Latin America, East Asia, and industrial countries; no SSA cases are discussed, even though well-established financing schemes have been in place in some African countries for decades. This treatment follows the general pattern in the literature—that is, most attention has focused on experience in other regions. In particular, the Latin American experience, in levying company payrolls to fund the building up of national training capacity under the aegis of representative national training bodies, has been well documented (CINTERFOR/ILO 1990, Ducci 1997). Similarly, in Asia, the Korean system of training-tax exemption, Singapore's levy-grant scheme, and Malaysia's changing funding system have all been closely studied.

But can these practices be applied in the very different African setting? The efficacy of relying too freely on institutional and policy "borrowing," particularly across continents, has been much questioned in recent years, both in relation to training and other policy areas (Keep 1991, Noble 1997, Ryan 1991). Differences in institutions, administrative capabilities, and cultural norms all militate against successful institutional and policy transfer across countries, especially where these differences are likely to be as substantial as between SSA countries and those in Latin America and Asia.

Of course, important lessons for policy may be learned from international experience; but these lessons are likely to be more relevant where gleaned from practical examples drawn from countries in SSA. For this reason, the general methodology adopted in this paper is to attempt to learn from internal SSA experience rather than from afar, and virtually all the country cases discussed are drawn from the region. Thus, the paper emphasizes the examination of particular financing mechanisms in those SSA countries where they are in place. Scattered documentation on training finance in SSA countries, contained mainly in government and donor agency reports, has been reviewed (where available) and analyzed comparatively.

This documentation for SSA countries, however, is mainly descriptive rather than analytical. Little evaluation work has been conducted—one reason being the relatively short time periods that have ensued since these mechanisms were instituted in many countries, although a more general disinclination in the region to carry out the necessary evaluative studies is evident. Yet, in examining these institutions, we need to know not only how they work but also how *well* they work. To this end, three short field studies were conducted in preparation for this paper, to South Africa, Tanzania, and Zimbabwe. The findings of these visits, and lessons learned, are reported at relevant points throughout the paper.

Coverage

The financing of training is, inherently, a wide topic. In this paper, we limit our coverage of the topic to training recipients, training providers, and the timing of training.

Training for whom?

Any realistic discussion of the financing of national training systems must take account of segmentation in the employment of skilled workers and resulting differences in financing needs. In this paper, we adopt the three-way classification of training for formal sector employment, training for the informal sector, and the training needs of special, targeted groups.

Most of the training finance literature, reflecting the emphasis and direction of training policy, has addressed the needs of the modern sector, notably of government employment or in public and private enterprises. But in SSA, as in other developing regions, this formal employment sector accounts for a relatively small part of total employment and displays little growth potential. In almost all African economies, the majority of the labor force remains attached to the informal sector, which includes employment in small-scale firms (microenterprises), nonprofessional self-employment, and most casual workers (ILO 1972). It is largely within this sector that the ever-growing potential labor force might expect to be absorbed into productive employment. Finally, the focused needs of a variety of specially targeted groups have received increasing public attention in recent years. For a range of reasons, which include meeting equity, political, and social objectives, governments have usually assumed responsibility for meeting the skills needs of these groups, which include the long-term unemployed, school dropouts, the disabled, poor and underprivileged groups (including urban and rural women), and socially excluded minorities.

Training by whom?

Training providers may be categorized in many ways. In this paper, we recognize three broad modes of training: (a) training in public training centers (usually under the aegis of ministries of labor), (b) private propriety training institutions, and (c) on-the-job training in companies. Vocational and technical education provided by the formal school system, and generally attached to ministries of education, is another component of what is usually referred to as the VET (vocational, education, and training) system. The financing of school-based vocational education is only obliquely covered in this paper. This omission may be problematic for discussions of the working of the VET system as a whole, including such issues as alternative modes of provision and cost-effectiveness. Unit costs at vocational schools generally far exceed those at general schools (Tsang 1997), while vocational schooling usually fails to produce superior labor market outcomes. Since this paper is not concerned with cost-benefit issues, however, the omission seems to be in order. There do not appear to be any major financing issues that relate to vocational schools, as such. The distinct financing issues relevant to vocational education are generally common to secondary schooling, rather than to training.

Timing: preemployment, initial, and continuing training

Finally, we consider the timing of training and distinguish between training received at the outset of workforce entry (preemployment training and initial training received on the job) and continuing training acquired over the working life (Jager and Buhrer 2000).

Preemployment training, generally acquired at formal training institutions prior to entering the labor market, provides skills for future employment and for generating income in self-employment. This preemployment training is distinguished from *initial training*, or skills training received on the job in the early stages of employment with an employer, including, but not limited to, apprenticeship in the formal and informal sectors. Continuing training, acquired on the job or at training institutions over the working career, may focus on updating existing skills (refresher courses) to avoid obsolescence and enhance productivity, on upgrading skills for new tasks and responsibilities, or on retraining, in response to technical and structural changes.

Plan of the paper

The paper follows a progression from more theoretical and conceptual issues (Chapters 2 and 3) to the more applied (Chapters 5 through 10), relating to SSA experience in training finance. Chapter 4, which maps out typical financing flows in training markets, provides a bridge between the conceptual and practical divisions of the paper.

Following this introduction, Chapter 2 begins with the conventional pattern of training finance, as found in many SSA countries today. We discuss how these conventional financing patterns (and particularly government's role in providing training) are proving inappropriate to meet the changing needs of the economy and society. Chapter 3 picks up on a major theme of the preceding chapter, discussing the appropriate roles of the state in financing and providing training. Chapter 4 examines typical training finance flows, from finance source to training provider. We do so for three construct training markets representing different stages on the continuum of development from conventional training finance to the type of integrated, demand-driven training markets regarded as best practice.

The paper then proceeds to practical issues, illustrated by SSA country experience. Chapters 5 and 6, respectively, select for in-depth analysis the two most pervasive institutional developments in the training finance arena: national training funds and training levies. Chapter 7 explores alternative sources of training finance and the efficacy of measures to augment funding by finance diversification. An analysis of funding transfer mechanisms is presented in Chapter 8, while Chapter 9 discusses mechanisms available for enhancing enterprise investments in training. Special financing issues related to training for the informal sector are discussed in Chapter 10.

While most of the paper is framed in positive terms—offering description and analysis of training finance systems and mechanisms presently in place in the region-the goal of the paper is to draw lessons from current experience to improve policies. In this spirit, each of the practical chapters—5 through 10—concludes with a summary discussion that provides practical advice for policy, including what measures work well, advantages and weaknesses of policy alternatives, and pitfalls to avoid in implementation. Chapter 11 deals with the interplay between national training policy objectives and the main mechanisms for training finance. The concluding chapter consolidates the main policy messages of the paper.

Notes

1 A summary, updated version is given in Ducci (1997).

2 A revised version appears as Chapter 4, in Middleton, Ziderman, and Adams (1993).

3 A shorter, revised version is available in Dougherty and Tan (1997).

4 See Lauglo (1992) and Bennell (1996).

CHAPTER 2

Conventional Patterns of Financing Training

Typology of financing burdens

Today, as in the past, the vast majority of employment across SSA countries is found within small-scale, informal sector enterprises (Table 2.1, Column 1). Traditionally, initial training for the informal sector took place on the job, within the context of the traditional, unstructured apprenticeship, with trainees (or their families) bearing the costs of training in the form of an initial lump-sum payment or a low (apprentice) wage (Table 2.1, Cell A1). This form of apprenticeship training, consisting largely of the handing down of initial skills for the semiskilled and craft trades, is usually a "one-off" activity; subsequently, very little continuing training takes place. Private (for-profit) training institutions provide an additional, although secondary, source of initial skills acquisition for the informal sector and small-scale businesses; enrolled students pay full-cost fees (Cell A2). Church and other nonprofit voluntary training institutions may provide free or highly subsidized initial training.

Formal sector training displays a different financing pattern (Table 2.1, Column 2). Where initial training provides general, transferable skills, the trainee-apprentice bears the cost of training through low wages (Becker 1964). To the extent that training is not transferable—perhaps because some skills are specific to the firm or because training markets are not competitive—the enterprise assumes some of the burden of financing initial training. Similar considerations apply to continuing training provided by the enterprise, with cost sharing between the worker and the firm reflecting the extent to which skills are transferable (Cell A2). Training in preemployment skills, acquired privately at proprietary training institutions, is paid for by students. Continuing training at these private training institutions may be financed by both the enterprise and the worker, or individually by one of the parties, again depending on the potential for transferring skills. To a lesser extent, subsidized initial training may be provided at voluntary training institutions.

All of these forms of training take place within private markets and are essentially demand-driven, focused on meeting market demands for skills. Yet, these traditional private markets have proved to be too limited to meet the broader skill needs for economic development and growth. Thus, nearly all developing countries have established parallel public training systems and, in most countries, the state has become a major player in training markets. It is a leading supplier of structured, preemployment training provided in public training centers (as well as in vocational schools), to the extent that it frequently dominates the market for training (mainly for the formal sector but also for informal sector employment). The state is also a major financier of preemployment training (Table 2.1, Row C); courses at public training sectors are either provided free or at purely nominal fees. Continuing training at public training centers is also usually highly subsidized, though enterprises may pay up to full costs for sponsored training or specialized courses at public training centers.

There has been much debate about the rationale for state intervention in training markets, in both the provision and the financing of training, particularly in relation to training for the formal sector. The strongest case for government provision of training can be made when private institutional training capacity is weak, inefficient, or underdeveloped. However, it is harder to make the case for the blanket supply of state-subsidized training—without payment or at nominal fees only—even though many countries around the world follow this pattern. We return to this issue in Chapter 3.

The arguments are somewhat reversed for the provision of training for special target groups at government training centers (Cell C3). Governments have increasingly assumed responsibility for improving the conditions of socially disadvantaged groups in the population. Seeing skills acquisition as a valuable tool for achieving these aims, many governments have responded

Table 2.1 Conventional Patterns of Financing Training in SSA

	Employment Sector		
	1	2	3
Training Provider	Informal Sector	Formal Sector	Special Groups
A Employers:			
Initial training (on-the-job) —Apprenticeship	Trainee financed	Trainee/Enterprise financed	—
Continuing training	—	Enterprise/Worker financed	—
B Private Institutions:			
Pre-employment training	Student financed	Student financed	—
Continuing training	—	Enterprise/Worker financed	—
C Public:			
Pre-employment training	State financed	State financed	—
Continuing training	—	State/Enterprise financed	State financed

— Not applicable or of limited importance.

by providing free training courses, often specially designed, for these at-risk groups. Indeed, a strong case can be made, on social grounds, for using public funds to subsidize the training of these groups; however, government training *delivery* is less clearly justified, particularly where alternative private training provision is in place or could be developed.

Shortcomings of conventional training financing

The simple financing framework outlined in Table 2.1, still current in many developing countries, has become inadequate to meet society's skill development needs. A number of emerging trends, which include but are not confined to those listed below, have rendered this framework outmoded.

- In many training systems there has been a tendency toward market failure, with firms undertraining, particularly in transferable skills. This is true both in terms of the amount of training provided and its quality. The presence of labor market distortions, such as overly narrow wage differentials, leading to weak incentives for workers to acquire skills, is prevalent in many developing economies. The risk that workers trained in both general and specific skills may move to other firms—as well as the strong incentives for firms to poach trained workers rather than invest in training their own work forces—may lead firms to underprovide training, thereby causing chronic shortages of well-trained, skilled workers in the formal sector. This in turn stunts productivity growth, competitiveness, and industrial development. Governments may intervene with corrective measures, often a combination of financial incentives and compulsion, to increase the quantity and quality of enterprise-provided training.

- In many countries technological change, structural adjustment policies, new and changing patterns of trade and competition, and globalization have created the need for a much more flexible and responsive training system for the modern sector. These ensuing changes lead to continuing, and more substantial, changes in skills demands in the labor market; but the more changeable the market demand for skills, the more flexible must be the supply response from the training system. Training systems for the formal sector are failing to respond to these emerging external challenges, mainly because they are too static, in a number of senses: First, training horizons are limited. Preemployment and initial training for the formal sector have concentrated too much on one-time learning for immediate employment. But the dynamics of labor markets and changing skill needs over the working life require a forward-looking approach, emphasizing future trainability in addition to the skill needs of immediate employment. Similarly, enterprises are largely reactive (focusing more on immediate needs) rather than being proactive in relation to investing in continuing training. Second, the institutional environment within which public training systems operate, with accountability to a government ministry, often results in training that is largely isolated from market forces; is subject to slowly changing, centralized curriculum decisions; and is circumscribed by limited institutional autonomy. Such public training systems, widely referred to as supply-driven, are unlikely to respond to the changing skill needs of a growing, competitive economy. These shortcomings may be overcome by the adoption of carefully selected training finance policies, with an appropriate blend of incentives, of compulsion, and of mechanisms to change the competitiveness of the training environment.
- Fiscal restraint is a central feature of structural adjustment policies introduced in many developing economies. Increasingly, limited public

sector budgets have seriously constrained the ability of governments to provide adequate and stable funding to the public training sector. In other economies, parsimonious public budgets result from the heavy reliance on revenues from indirect taxes, such as domestic excise taxes falling on a narrow range of commodities, and taxes on internationally traded goods. Broadening the tax base to include the direct taxation of personal income, as in industrial economies, may not be feasible in many developing countries: not only is formal sector employment relatively small, but there are difficulties in taxing the urban sector and the large and widely scattered rural population. Pressures on the central budget and the lack of constant and adequate funding for public sector training has led to the identification and tapping of alternative sources of funding, including a greater degree of cost sharing among the beneficiaries of training programs.

- In many developing countries, demographic change and high population growth rates have resulted in substantial increases in the numbers of those entering the labor force. For Africa, it is estimated that labor force entries will continue to outnumber departures by a factor of three (Wander 1987). The result has been high unemployment, underemployment, and low wages, especially for a country's youth. Since in many SSA countries, the modern employment sector remains small and stagnant with little potential for expansion over the medium to long term, an expanding urban informal sector is becoming a major source of manpower absorption and employment growth. These trends will require a redirection of training toward meeting the needs of informal sector development, in terms of job skills provision and entrepreneurial skills.

- There is an increasing social awareness (and conscience) about the low status and lack of skills of the poor, ethnic minorities, and women. In parallel, there is a wider sense that the government is obligated to help, through financing and perhaps skills provision; yet these groups are likely to succeed in securing employment only though posttraining entry to the informal sector. However, increasingly limited public budgets and greater intersectoral competition for funding will severely limit the amount of government funding for these developments. This may indicate an appropriate role for donor intervention.

Changing roles for the state, enterprises, and individuals

To meet these challenges, training systems in many countries, and the ways in which they are financed, will need to adapt to the new realities. This, in turn, will require a reexamination of the current roles of the state, enterprises, and individuals in training markets and how these roles will need to change. Directions of change will include the development of private training markets, increased competition between public and private training providers, declining roles for the state in the financing and provision of training, a greater diversification of funding sources for skills development (including enhanced cost recovery, cost sharing, and training levies), the encouragement of more and higher quality enterprise training, and meeting the needs of the informal sector. In subsequent chapters, these themes will be developed and applied to the SSA context. That discussion, however, is supported by the two more conceptually based chapters that follow.

CHAPTER 3

The Role of the State in Financing

Training

Funding mechanisms are aimed in part at augmenting the supply of training resources. As noted, in conventional training markets it is the state, rather than the direct beneficiaries, that bears the major burden in the financing of training for the formal sector, particularly preemployment training. Thus, reaching out to new sources of training finance would usually entail lightening the government's finance burden (either in the funding of the current training system or its expansion). Indeed, this is often the motivation for diversifying sources of finance through cost shifting to other actors. Cost shifting may also be in order in situations where government funding of training is thought to be excessive. But are existing levels of state funding of training excessively high? Before considering any measures to reduce this financing burden (in relative or absolute terms), it is fitting to look at the factors that may justify government financing of training. Against this background, the appropriate role for governmental intervention in financial training markets may be more readily assessed.

Discussion of the appropriate role and level of government intervention in the financing of training is frequently confounded by the double role assumed by government in many training markets—it acts both as training provider and training financier. The clearest example is government provision of preemployment training, without charge, at public training centers.

But these dual functions are not inextricably linked. The state could finance similar training at private training institutions, or could charge full-cost fees for the courses it provides.

Rationale for government intervention

This chapter examines seven major arguments for justifying a government role in financing or provision of training, which are summarized in Table 3.1. The table builds on an earlier formulation (Ziderman 1990), which formed a central focus of the approach to these issues presented in the World Bank policy paper on vocational education and training (World Bank 1991).[1]

External benefits

Of the arguments for a public role in training, the government response is clearest in the case of market failures in the form of "externalities." Positive externalities exist where the benefits of training that accrue to society exceed the private benefits realized by trainees and firms. Thus, from a societal perspective, the decisions of trainees and firms will lead to a shortfall of spending on training. For example, the shortages of a particular skill might inhibit the development of a new industry that is strategic for growth. Wages offered for these, potentially bottleneck, skills may not reflect the future social benefits that the employment of these skilled workers will provide, with the result that shortages of the new skill impedes the development of the strategic new industry. This version of market failure justifies training subsidies but not necessarily provision (Table 3.1). The cost of subsidizing training may be legitimately drawn from general taxation on the grounds that society as a whole benefits (via its externality effects) from the extra skills generated.

This type of externality argument, often advanced to justify general education subsidies, is generally less strong for training, which may be more narrowly focused on providing skills relevant to particular occupations. Apart from the potential bottleneck type of argument advanced above, the more narrowly conceived is the training, the fewer are the wider societal benefits it will provide, and the weaker is the case for

Table 3.1 Policy Options for Public Intervention in Training Markets

Reason for intervention	State subsidy of training	State provision of training		Complementary policies
	Policy Options			
Externalities	P	N	—	None
Property rights	A	N	P	Levy-grant schemes
Market imperfections	A	N	P	Deal with sources of market imperfections*
Inadequate enterprise training	A	N	P	Build up enterprise training capacity Levy-grant schemes
Weak private training provision	N	A/P	P	Build up private institutional training capacity
Parity	A	N	P	Reduce subsidies to trainees' peer groups, together with introduction of selective scholarships
Disadvantaged groups	P	N	P	Targeted training subsidies Employment creation Income redistribution

Notes: P = Preferred policy approach; A = Acceptable (second-best) approach; N = Policy not justified; * = Policies may not be feasible

public subsidy. A major problem with this traditional externality argument is ascertaining the appropriate size of the justified subsidy, given the elusive nature of many of these externality benefits and the notorious difficulties associated with their measurement. There is always the danger of costly oversubsidization of training.

Property rights

The presence of externalities constitutes the classic form of market failure, justifying government financial intervention in such markets. We now turn to a different form of market failure that is particularly relevant to training markets. Unlike company investment in capital assets, such as plant and machinery, firms do not have property rights over the human capital created by training that is vested in their workers. This may give rise to the "poaching problem"—that is, the tendency for firms to recruit (or poach) workers trained in transferable skills from other firms, rather than train their own employees. Poaching imposes costs on firms that train because of the loss of newly trained workers to poaching firms. Training firms will then cut down on their training efforts or offer training that is narrow and not readily transferable—that is, training that is unlikely to yield externalities or carry a high societal return (Katz and Ziderman 1990). The result is a general underprovision of trained workers.

The preferred policy is the introduction of levy-grant schemes, based on payroll levies, and thus not requiring government finance (discussed more fully in Chapter 9). The rationale of levy-grant schemes is the cross-subsidization of training firms, financed by the levy paid by non-training firms (potential poachers). Corrective government subsidies, offering training incentives to firms, may be acceptable (as a "second-best" solution), particularly where externality benefits might accrue; but there is no justification for government training provision.

Market imperfections

If training markets work imperfectly, the result may be underinvestment in training. A major source of training market imperfections stems from unintended side effects of economic and social policies that distort incentives for individuals and enterprises to invest in training. Government wage policies that result in the compression of wage differentials for equity reasons provide an example of these policies. This compression reduces private incentives to acquire skills. The preferred solution is for the government to address the policy source of the market imperfection, but this may not be desirable or politically feasible. It that case, government intervention in the financing of training to offset the imperfection may be justified; the subsidies could take the form of training grants to individuals or subsidizing enterprise training. The aim of the training subsidy would be to restore a positive balance between the private benefits and costs of training, so that incentives for private investments in skills acquisition remain sufficiently high.

Inadequate enterprise training

Enterprises may be reluctant to discharge their training role. Nonprofit-maximizing behavior by firms may lead them to undertrain. Managerial lethargy, a noncompetitive production environment, and a lack of company foresight are reasons that companies may fail to organize structured in-service training, particularly apprenticeship training. This gap, however, does not make a case for government training provision. While subsidies may be useful as an incentive to companies to build up training capacity (including the subsidy of apprenticeship wages), more proactive approaches are preferred, particularly over the long term. These approaches include both the offering to firms of training advisory services and technical assistance by government (or by a national training fund) to improve training capacities, and the incentives provided by levy-grant schemes.

Weak private training provision

In countries where the modern sector is underdeveloped and the size of enterprises is small, there may be an insufficient enterprise base to provide the capacity for structured, low-cost training. This situation would open the way for the growth of private, specialized training institutions. Yet, such initiatives may not be forthcoming, particularly in lower-income countries, because of a lack of expertise, capital shortages, and constraining regulatory policies of government. Here, the public sector may perform a critical role in meeting skill needs. But government provision is seen best in terms of performing a transitional role, as government encourages and facilitates the developing of private training capacity; this would then complement and provide a more competitive framework for training provision by the public sector.

Parity

The final two arguments are concerned with social issues. The first relates to the heavy subsidies given to secondary schooling and tertiary education in many countries. These are a source of social inequity, particularly when the beneficiaries come from privileged backgrounds. Here the parity argument for extending subsidies to individuals undergoing training is quite strong (in the case where trainee peer group subsidies cannot be reduced substantially), particularly where preemployment training is directed toward less privileged individuals.

Disadvantaged groups

The second social argument concerns the training needs of disadvantaged groups in society, for whom training is regarded as an important tool for improving their incomes and employability. As noted in Chapter 2, there exists a broad consensus, matched by practice in many countries, that it is government's task to ensure that these needs are met. These special programs are financed out of the public purse through the provision of courses at public training institutions. While public finance of these training programs is justified, public delivery is less so—particularly where alternative private training provision is available or could be developed.

Designing appropriate policy interventions

Conditions for government intervention in training markets are present in virtually all countries. However, because the economic environments, which shape the incentives for employers and individuals to invest in training, differ across countries and are subject to change, there can be no single prescription for policy on state intervention in training markets. Rather, the role of governments in the provision and financing of training has to be based on local conditions and informed by careful economic analysis. The policy matrix provided in Table 3.1 serves as a checklist for probing the justification for training market intervention policies in a given country situation.

What conclusions for policy in SSA countries may be drawn from this discussion? We note three central conclusions for policy.

The first is that the appropriate role of government in training markets is to let private training markets work where they function well and, where they do not, to engage the public sector. This definition of the government role in financing and providing training requires a country to determine its own needs for public sector training intervention. It will need to examine the performance of its training markets, the capacity of the private sector to deliver training, and its own preferences toward social policies and equity. On this basis, the state is likely to maintain a continuing role in many countries in the delivery and, particularly, in the financing of training.

The second is that there is probably much more public *provision* of training than is required by economic rationale alone. But this may not be suboptimal if public training is efficient, effective, and market-responsive. Unfortunately, this is often not the case. An important task of funding disbursement policies, as discussed in Chapter 8, is to provide an appropriate mix of regulation and incentives to ensure public training can hold its own in an environment of competitive training markets.

Third, it seems that there is far more public *financing* of training than is justified by the economic arguments above. Given the increasing pressures on government budgets, this conclusion provides an opening for funding diversification—a major theme of this paper.

Notes

1 See also the discussion in Middleton, Ziderman, and Adams (1993); a technical presentation is provided in Katz and Ziderman (1999).

CHAPTER 4

Finance Flows: Three Scenarios

Much of the literature on training finance mechanisms does not do a good job of putting these mechanisms into context. In particular, not enough attention is given to showing how various mechanisms interreact and how they relate to the existing training financing system as a whole. This chapter places the subsequent discussion of particular financing mechanisms within a broader framework of the overall system of training finance.

We discuss three broad scenarios, corresponding to progressively higher levels of maturation of training finance systems. The first relates to traditional training finance flows in conventional training markets, as discussed in the previous chapter: a bureaucratic, government-financed and -controlled public sector, providing preemployment training, coexists with private training markets for informal and enterprise training. We then proceed to training markets where the state still exerts a powerful influence on training for the formal sector, but of a different kind. Now the state acquires a stronger role in regulating the financing system through earmarked training levies (particularly in relation to enterprise-provided training)—but where parsimony in state financing of public training institutions brings about increased financial diversification of public training. Third, we look at modern, integrated financing systems, displaying strong moves toward competitive, demand-driven training markets. These scenarios are presented as synthetic constructs to guide our understanding of policy development, rather than actual, delineated stages in the evolution of training systems. Not every country will fall neatly into one of the three categories; some country situations will span across categories.

Conventional training markets

We first consider major finance flows in conventional training markets, as reflected in the presentation in Table 2.1. A schematic overview is presented in Figure 4.1. The white boxes indicate institutions that provide training. As noted, training may be provided through private training markets either by firms or in proprietary training institutions; it may also be provided within the public sector at public training institutions. However, the training market is fragmented into two distinct sectors—private and public.

The major training providers in the private sector are enterprises and proprietary training institutions. The private training sector is market-driven, unsubsidized, and usually competitive. Firms in both the informal and formal employment sectors provide training to trainees/workers in their employ; payment is made by the employee/trainee through initial lump-sum fee or implicitly in the form of low, below-productivity wages. Individuals enroll in preemployment courses, at full fees, in private training institutions; training fees for continuing training may be borne partially by formal sector employers.

In contrast, public sector training institutions are predominantly financed by government. Where they are current, student fees are set at purely nominal levels and often accrue to the government rather than remaining with institutions. Firms may enroll their workers for continuing training courses, provided at full cost but more usually at subsidized fee levels. Because budget allocations to public training providers are usually ad hoc and unrelated to objective, outcome measures—such as success in placing trainees in productive employment—there is little incentive for training providers to align their training courses with the needs of the labor market. Linkages between public training centers and formal sector employers remain poor; training provision is mostly supply-driven. Moreover, training centers do not develop training programs focusing on the particular needs of informal sector employment, nor do they cater to the special needs of minority and disadvantaged groups.

There are many SSA examples of this scenario, including Ethiopia, Mozambique, and Zambia. These financing markets display many of the traditional shortcomings that training finance—and more general—reforms aim at correcting. Zambia is now in a process of training policy and finance reform; this will move it strongly in the direction of the second scenario, which we now discuss.

Training markets with state intervention

While such conventional training markets remain in place in many African countries, others show strong evidence of moving away from these traditional forms of training finance and provision. The driving force behind these moves has been the increased intervention of the state in training markets; paradoxically, this process has involved a *retreat* by the state in financing training. Increasing pressures on government budgets in general, and on public training budgets in particular, has initiated a search for additional or alternative sources of funding for training. In addition to the need to tap nongovernment sources of funding, governments have intervened more strongly in training markets in order to counter shortcomings of conventional private training markets and notably the tendency for enterprises to undertrain.

Figure 4.1. Finance Flows: Traditional Fragmented Training Markets

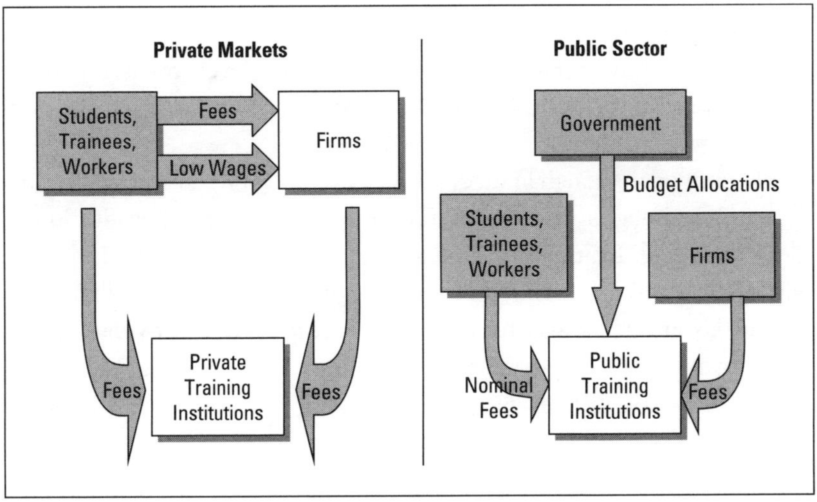

The process of funding diversification has taken a number of forms. By far the most important has been increased sharing of the costs of public sector training by other training beneficiaries, notably firms and workers. Figure 4.2 shows the major financing flows.

In many countries throughout the world, special taxes earmarked for supporting training have been adopted—indicated by (1) in the figure. The predominant format has been a percentage levy on company payrolls. Payroll levies offer a means of mobilizing funds for training that are otherwise inaccessible to the public sector. First introduced in Brazil in the 1940s, payroll levies have become an important alternative to government budgetary allocations to the public training sector in many developing countries, as well as in a number of industrial economies. In these cases, cost sharing is the rationale underlying the imposition of payroll levies, which generate revenues for the support of public training. Firms are the partial, though indirect, beneficiaries of publicly provided training, in terms of a better-trained workforce, enhanced productivity levels, and greater profits, and therefore should share in its costs.

More cost sharing may also be achieved by raising course fees at public training institutions. We have noted that such training is traditionally provided free, or at purely nominal fee levels, in many developing countries. But trainees are the major and direct beneficiaries of these training programs, in terms of improved employability, greater productivity, and higher incomes, whether from wage- or self-employment. This indicates that greater cost recovery through the imposition of more realistic, albeit still subsidized, trainee fees—item (2) in Figure 4.2—is both justified and feasible. However, the raising of fee levels for public training may need to be accompanied by selective scholarships for the poor and disadvantaged.

An additional, though limited, source of funding diversification for public sector training is income generation by public training institutions—(3) in the figure. Examples are the generation of income from production within the training context, and the hiring out of underutilized facilities. Finally, governments may turn to donor institutions to provide funding, either to the government or directly to individual training institutions (4). In some country settings, donor funding constitutes an important source of financing for public sector training institutions.

Figure 4.2. Finance Flows: Training Markets with Strong State Intervention

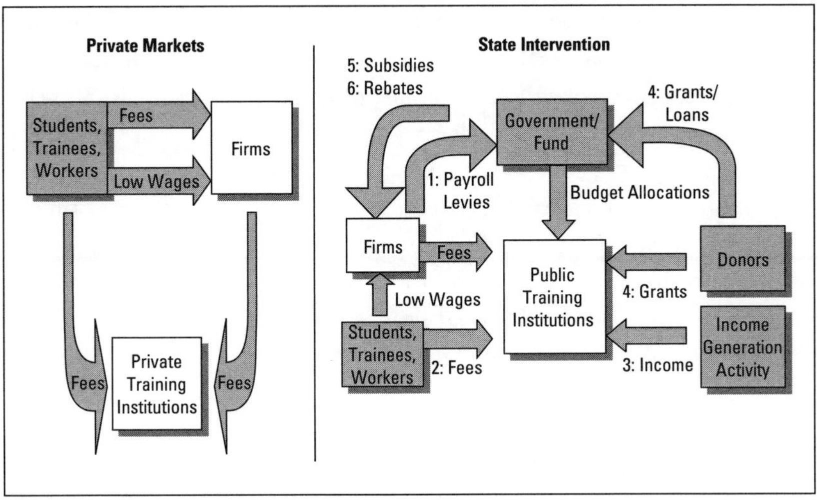

A second major reason for government intervention in conventional training markets is a corrective one: to encourage formal sector enterprises to provide more and better training. Governments subsidize enterprise training, either directly from central government budget appropriations or, less usually, from specially designated training funds, also financed fully or in part by government—(5) in Figure 4.2. But tight public budgets may limit the government's ability to subsidize enterprise training from public funds. Levy-grant schemes, based on payroll taxes, have provided governments in many developing countries with an alternative mechanism for promoting company training. Unlike the "revenue-generating" rationale for payroll levies discussed above—where the revenues from training levies are earmarked to finance public sector training institutions—levy-grant schemes are directed toward training provided by enterprises. While many variants are found in terms of actual practice, the common feature of levy-grant schemes is the provision of incentives for firms to provide more and better training. Payroll levies are often linked to reimbursement mechanisms, whereby firms receive payments related to the amount of designated forms of training they provide—(6) in Figure 4.2. Payroll tax revenues are distributed as rebates, usually up to a specified percentage of the tax paid, to firms that set up or broaden programs of in-service training.

One outcome of the introduction and spread of earmarked training levies has been the development of a relatively new type of financing mechanism—the national training fund. These funds usually constitute both the depository of collected training levies and the mechanism for their distribution. Government budgetary allocations may supplement levy income to the fund, or represent its major income source; donor support is important in some cases. The intention is to provide a sheltered funding source for national training development, including the financing of public sector training, the provision of incentives for enterprise training, and meeting the skill needs of special groups. Training funds usually operate outside normal government budgetary channels; thus, they are more readily accessed and may be utilized more flexibly than would normally be the case with direct government-financed training programs. Operating as they do under varying degrees of autonomy from government control, however, a fund's freedom of maneuver may be constrained. Thus, in cases where the degree of independence from ministry of labor and treasury control is limited, the funds may emerge as conservative, reactive bodies, rather than proactive and independent in fund policy and management.

Overall, this stage may be one that strengthens the market orientation of the training system. The emphasis is on government intervention in training markets rather than on direct government financing and control. There is a strong move toward diversification of training finance. Drake and Germe (1994) note that an element in this shift "is to change the means of raising funds from general taxation, by definition unrelated to training or to structural shifts within the economy, towards dedicated taxation like payroll taxes."

The training finance system currently in place in Zimbabwe is an example of this scenario; it illustrates certain weaknesses associated with the financing systems typical of this scenario. Recent training reform legislation in Tanzania is moving that county's training financing system toward scenario 3. Both cases will be discussed subsequently.

Integrated, demand-driven training markets

The training finance mechanisms now in place in many SSA countries conform broadly to the schema set out in Figure 4.2. But these training finance systems suffer from two major shortcomings. First, public training provision remains essentially supply-driven. It is not subject to the discipline of competition with other training providers; nor are guidance mechanisms in place for matching the skills supplied by public training institutions with the skill needs of the market. Second, and related to this, while the training finance system is more integrated than that illustrated in Figure 4.1 (with formal sector enterprise-based training, as well as public sector training, now subject jointly to policies of state intervention), much fragmentation remains. In particular, private training institutions do not operate within the same financing framework as public sector training providers. Corrective mechanisms have been introduced in a number of countries; these are shown in Figure 4.3, which relates to training finance flows in more integrated, demand-driven training markets.

In many countries, national training agencies or authorities (NTAs) form the linchpin of the financing system. NTAs may be attached, with varying degrees of autonomy, to a government department (usually the labor ministry), but they are likely to operate more effectively as largely autonomous bodies forming a buffer between government and the training system. Boards representing the training system's major stakeholders usually run them. While most NTAs receive general government funding, a large number are financed solely or additionally by payroll levies. NTAs are much broader in scope than training funds, and are usually empowered with a wide range of national training responsibilities. In addition to managing the system of enterprise training subsidies and—where levy-grant systems are in place—levy reimbursements, NTAs may be responsible for developing national training policies and standards, planning the national training system, accreditation of institutions, and generating and disseminating relevant labor market information.

NTAs may be better placed than environmentally constrained government departments to operate payment mechanisms for training institutions in ways that promote efficiency and competitiveness in training markets—(1) in Figure 4.3. Normative financing replaces the largely ad hoc budgeting of training institutions. Formula funding of public training institutions (such as output-related funding) provides one example of such measures. Contracted training, particularly to meet the needs of disadvantaged groups, is another. Based on competitive tender that is open to public and

Figure 4.3. Finance Flows: Integrated, Demand-Driven Training Markets

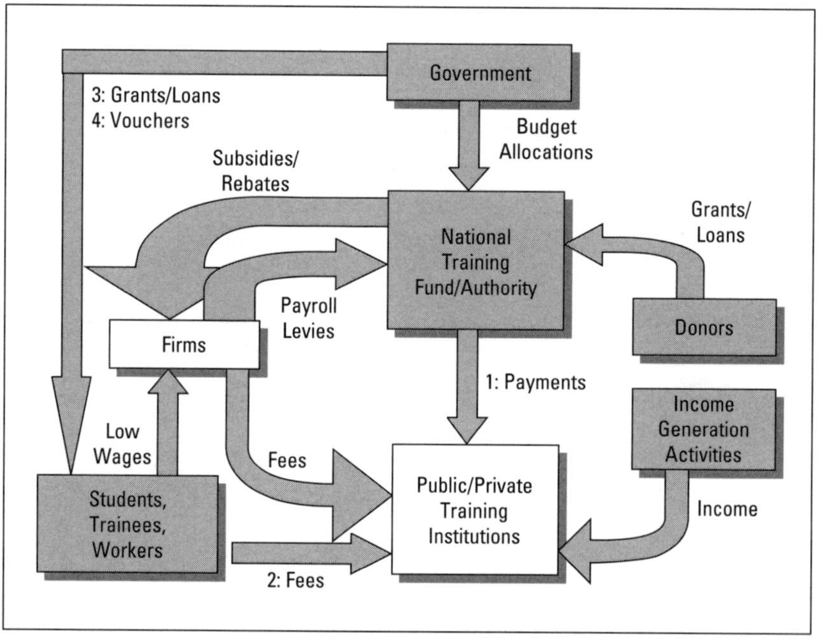

private training institutions, contracted training can, through the bidding process, both integrate training markets and pressure public training institutions to be more efficient and to operate at lower cost. In line with this approach, donor agencies would fund the NTA only, not individual training institutions.

In parallel, other moves toward more open, competitive markets may be taken. Fees at public training institutions may be raised closer to competitive levels (2), facilitated by the availability of selective scholarships for the poor or student/trainee loans (3). The introduction of a supportive policy framework to help develop and expand private training provision complements this approach. Vouchers may be made available to potential trainees to purchase training in the open market, with public and private training providers competing for trainee enrollments (4).

Recent training finance reforms in South Africa, which are currently being implemented, provide an example of a system moving strongly in the direction of scenario 3, though, notably, not in all aspects. The South African case will be discussed in detail at various points in the paper.

A broader role for sound financing mechanisms

A leading theme of this paper, underlined in the discussion in the present chapter, is the emphasis given to the broader role of sound financing mechanisms (beyond pure finance) in leading to effective, demand-driven training systems. A well-designed financing framework has a central, integrating role to play, beyond the traditional ones concerned with the sources and distribution of finance for training. Training finance mechanisms should be fashioned as an integrated system whose central role is to encourage and facilitate the transformation of fragmented, inefficient training systems (with underfunded, supply-driven public provision) into a nonfragmented, competitive, demand-oriented training market. In this chapter, we have emphasized five elements of this process:

- *Funding diversification,* with greater cost sharing (via more realistic training fees) and income generation by training institutions
- *Augmenting and improving enterprise training,* through subsidies, incentives, and levy rebates
- *Trainee-based funding,* through student grants, loans (and perhaps vouchers) leading to training that is more in keeping with market demands
- *Effective institutional financing,* replacing ad hoc institutional funding by normative funding methods
- *Integration of private and public training markets,* by such mechanisms as competitive bidding for the provision of government-sponsored training programs.

The pace of reform

These scenarios have been presented as successive stages in a process leading to the third scenario. Essentially, these stages can be seen as positions on a spectrum, ranging from government finance, provision, and control to integrated and free (or simulated) training markets.[1] We have also noted a consensus in the survey literature on training finance systems that argues strongly in favor of training financing systems displaying many of the characteristics of scenario 3. This should not be seen as suggesting that all SSA countries with "lower-stage" training finance systems should embark on drastic reforms leading to training finance systems resembling the third scenario. As Drake and Germe (1994) remind us: "... most financing innovations are regime modifications." Each country will need to advance at a pace consistent with its present stage of economic and social development, and which takes account of implementation constraints imposed by limitations in existing institutional and organizational capacity. This indeed is how "best practice" should be understood—as a relative rather than absolute concept, defined in terms of practices best suited to a country's stage of economic and institutional development.

Thus, some countries would need to advance more quickly on some aspects of financial reform than on others. For example, comprehensive plans for training finance reform in Zambia, as outlined in a government strategy paper (Ministry of Science, Technology and Vocational Training, Zambia 1997)—and which were in line with reform trends in other countries—included the imposition of a payroll levy to finance a national training fund. These plans have now been scaled down following second thoughts about what is feasible and capable of being implemented. In particular, levy financing of the training fund has been postponed to a later stage. In Madagascar, implementation of a payroll levy also was held back, while moving ahead with other funding reforms. Experience in Togo is instructive. With donor support, plans were developed to restructure the training system to be more demand-driven and responsive to the needs of the production sector. These plans proved to be overly ambitious, given the capacity of key institutions and the motivation of private sector actors, whose active participation was an essential ingredient for effective restructuring.

Notes

1 Drake (1991) also discusses financing modes in an evolutionary context. Focusing on training finance regimes in industrial West European economies, he identifies

four forms of market intervention along a continuum ranging from "pure bureaucracy to pure market." These are defined as market-displacing, market-supplementing, market-regulatory, and market-reliant modes. While our two approaches have commonalities, Drake's relates to training regimes in industrial economies, while the focus here is on training finance in developing countries. A somewhat dated, though still highly relevant, discussion of national training agencies is given in Herschbach (1990). A number of training fund case studies and a comparative analysis are provided in World Bank (1997).

CHAPTER 5

The Development of National Training Funds

Origins and objectives

Training funds are a central element in the training finance system in many countries throughout the world. Most SSA countries already employ them, and they are on the policy agenda in a number of others. Training funds constitute an institutional framework for allocating funding to training providers, and are usually concerned with enhancing the supply, quality, and relevance of training provision. Yet, not all training funds share the same objectives, have the same coverage, or operate in the same way. For a clearer understanding of how training funds work, they must be examined from a number of viewpoints—particularly in terms of their defined tasks, organizational structure, and sources of income and disbursements.

Training funds originate with the development of earmarked training levies. The earliest forms of training levies—assessed on the total payroll of enterprises—were developed in a number of Latin American countries, as an integral part of the working of employer-based national training boards. Levy income was designated mainly to fund public training institutions run by the training boards. The process was usually concerned with the collection and management of levy funding; a protected depository was required for the dedicated proceeds of the levy—hence, the growth of special training funds.

Training funds have since been developed in many countries. But the line of development has not been uniform, depending on differing historical origins, policy objectives, and the institutional framework. Some training funds are centrally concerned with funding disbursement to training providers—both training institutions and enterprises. Others constitute the disbursement arm of national training authorities/boards (to be considered later in this chapter), which are charged with broader national responsibilities, such as training provision, institutional accreditation, and national training policy. Some act as autonomous bodies, usually under the aegis of a usually tripartite advisory board; for others, freedom of independent action is constrained by ministerial control, often a ministry of labor. Most training funds receive their income from training levies, alone or in concert with funding from other sources, mainly government budgets or donor payments. In other cases, no training levies are in place, and government and donors remain the major income source. Some funds are empowered to provide funding to a wide range of training providers and forms of training; others are made responsible for a more limited part of the training spectrum.

Thus, the objectives—and therefore the range of activities—of training funds vary widely from case to case. "The characteristics of individual training agencies (funds) vary so greatly that it is difficult to generalize about them" (Herschbach 1990). Thus, the concept of "best practice" in relation to training funds is nebulous, given this heterogeneity in objectives and practice. Nevertheless, in the final section of this chapter, we do attempt to formulate a scenario that represents the growing consensus on the role of training funds and good practice. Before offering our prescription, we begin our discussion in positive terms.[1]

Range of activities

A national training fund may be seen as an institutional framework for unifying and augmenting public sources of funding for training and for allocating funds in line with national policies and priorities. Figure 5.1 indicates this range of activities. While in older, established training funds training levies were the dominant (usually only) income source, the figure emphasizes the variety of available income sources: government budgetary allocations, donor funding, and income generated by the fund itself. Indeed, in some cases the training fund derives no income from training levies; either levies have not been instituted or, where in place, levy proceeds are regarded, in practice, as general tax revenues and are not passed on to the fund.

On the disbursements side, the range of institutions and training forms eligible for funding support also may vary markedly from case to case. Earlier training funds based on payroll levies were largely single purpose—aimed at financing public sector preemployment training (revenue-generating schemes) or at enhancing the amount and quality of enterprise training investment (levy-grant schemes). There were some examples of mixed objectives; a case in point is the Nigerian Industrial Training Fund, which, at first only a levy-grant scheme, subsequently provided preemployment training at its vocational training centers. But in all these cases, levy income was not only committed to predesignated disbursement targets, but there was also a large degree of consonance between those who financed the levy and those receiving the benefits of the training—a theme we develop more fully in the next chapter.

With the broadening of training funds, both in terms of income sources and the allocation of disbursements, this link has been considerably weakened. Training funds are increasingly regarded as a general funding pool, distributed across various recipient destinations according to established priorities and policies. This often results in a considerable degree of cross-subsidization of training. Even in the new funding arrangements in South Africa, where business opposition to the imposition of a national payroll levy had been strong, a fifth of payroll levy income is being assigned to a central fund (supplemented by government allocations) to finance largely nonenterprise-related training.

Income sources

We have noted the strong connection traditionally between payroll levy systems and the development of training funds. Now, however, sources of income for training funds are notable for their diversity. The major income source of most training funds remains training levies, usually, but not invariably, levied on

Figure 5.1. National Training Funds: Framework of Activities

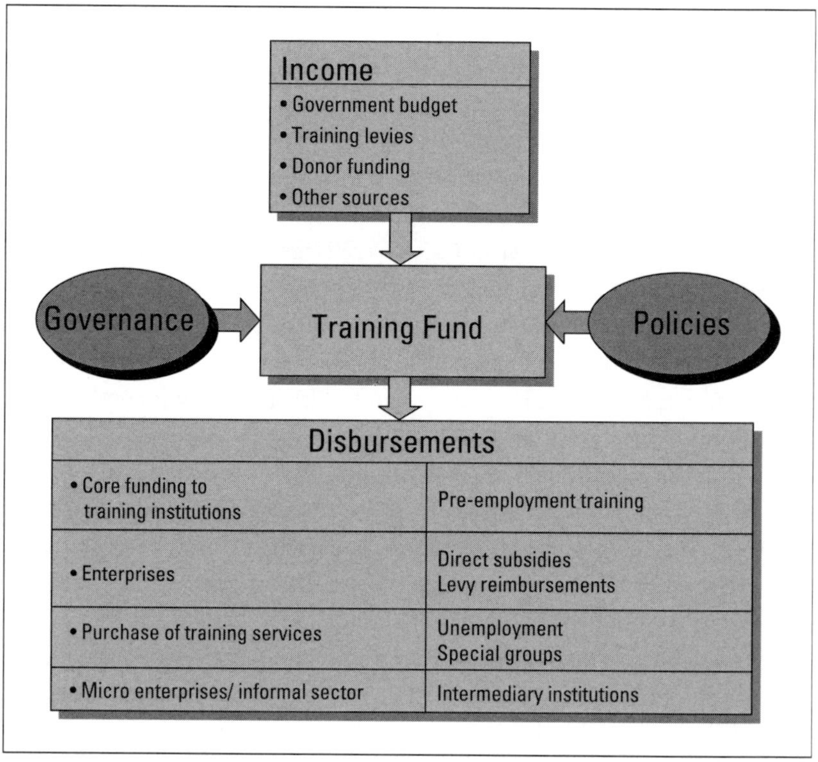

enterprise payrolls; however, government budgetary appropriations and donor funding are becoming more prominent, and some training funds may generate additional income from other activities. Where training levies are in place, they may be levied on a uniform basis (for example, a standard percentage of enterprise payrolls) or they may vary (say, across sectors). Once collected, levy proceeds are usually administered through a central fund; however, other arrangements may be preferred, such as the use of separate sectoral-based funds (discussed later in this chapter).

Country examples

Table 5.1, relating to eight different income source combinations in selected SSA countries, illustrates some of this diversity.

The Zimbabwe Manpower Development Fund (ZIMDEF) is, at least formally, typical of classic funding arrangements: a uniform, centrally administered payroll levy being the sole income source. More recently (as discussed below), ZIMDEF has benefited from considerable investment income derived from levy surpluses and real estate investments, an aberration from accepted practice.

The former Industrial Training Fund in Malawi (currently being replaced by a broader-based funding scheme) financed the national apprenticeship scheme through reimbursement of apprenticeship wages and grants to technical colleges. Training levies, again, were the sole funding source; they were in the form of a differentiated head tax on skilled workers, by skills category rather than a payroll levy. In Côte d'Ivoire and in Tanzania, levy income is supplemented by donor contributions and, in Côte d'Ivoire, by government funding. Formally, the National Training Fund in Togo is also financed by a payroll levy, the government, and donors; in practice the proceeds of the levy remain with the treasury and are not transferred to the fund.

The new funding system being established in South Africa is financed by a uniform 1 percent payroll levy. Eighty percent of proceeds are allocated to new sectoral training bodies (Sector Education and Training Authorities [SETAs]) for disbursement within their sectors. In Kenya, the Industrial Training Fund is funded by 11 separate sector-based training levies; separate sectoral accounts are kept with no cross-subsidization across sectors. In Madagascar, the training fund is financed by government and the International Development Association; while a payroll levy is planned, Madagascar now provides an example of a fund that is not financed by an earmarked training levy, whether based on payrolls or otherwise.

Disbursement

Figure 5.1 also shows the major destination categories for fund disbursement—sometimes referred to as "funding windows." Each of these four categories is aimed at distinct client groups (though there is some degree of classificatory overlap) representing an appropriate response to different training needs and policy objectives.

The first category shown is provision of core funding to training institutions for preemployment skills development, aimed largely at formal sector employment. As noted, government support of such training at public training institutions is a central element in conventional training markets; similarly, revenue-raising payroll levy schemes are supportive of this training. Training incentives may be offered to enterprises in the formal sector if initial training (including apprenticeship training) or continuing training is deemed insufficient (as discussed in Chapter 3). These incentives may take the form of direct training subsidies to companies or, where levy-grant schemes are in place, one of the levy reimbursement variants (discussed more fully in the following chapter).

The fund may also open a disbursement window to provide training courses for the unemployed and for disadvantaged groups. Traditionally, providing for the training needs of these groups has been seen as a government responsibility through the financing of courses at public training institutions. Contracting for the provision of such training, following public tender open to both public and private training providers, is now seen as the preferred method of finance intervention (see Chapter 8). Finally, meeting the training needs of microenterprises and the informal sector has in the past been largely relegated to the workings of private markets. But, as discussed in Chapter 2, these conventional private markets cannot meet the changing needs of this growing, more technological-based sector. It is now more common for training funds to offer financial incentives and subsidies for such training; for this, new financing mechanisms are being fashioned via the services of intermediary institutions (such as in Kenya). These themes are developed further in Chapter 10.

A given fund may not cover all of the purposes indicated in the Figure. The range of institutions and training forms eligible for support will usually be designated in the legislation (or other legal instrument) setting up the fund; this may be tightly defined or presented in general terms only. Which funding windows are in place and the relative size of disbursements made will depend on the parameters of each country setting. These parameters are related particularly to availability of income to the fund and to the country's training needs.

The situation in many SSA countries may differ from that in other regions, in turn requiring different disbursement policies. In many SSA countries, the precarious state of public budgets, combined with limited income-generating capacity of payroll levies, will require the government

Table 5.1 Income Sources of National Training Funds, Selected SSA Countries

		Major Source of Training Funds			
			Training Levy		
Country	Year Fund Established	Government Budget	Payroll Levy	Other Levy	Donor Support
Zimbabwe	1984	No	Uniform: Administered centrally	—	No
Malawi (currently being replaced)	1972	No	—	Uniform: Administered centrally	No
Côte d'Ivoire	1977, 1992	Yes	Uniform: Administered centrally	—	Yes
Tanzania	1994	Ceased	Uniform: Administered centrally	—	Yes
Togo	1988	Yes	Uniform: Not used for training	—	Yes
South Africa	1999	Yes	Uniform: Administered sectorally	—	Planned
Kenya	1971	No	—	Sector-based levies: Administered sectorally	No?
Madagascar	1992	Yes	Not at present but planned	—	Yes

(or the governing body of the fund) to decide on strict disbursement priorities. Indeed, the introduction of payroll levies may be premature because of administrative difficulties and the relatively small size of the formal employment sector; so the fund will rely more heavily on government allocations and perhaps donor support. Thus, for example, levy-grant schemes (with incentives for enterprise training) have been popular—and successful—in a number of Asian countries. In contrast, the relatively small size of the formal employment sector and its lack of growth, combined with considerable growth potential for informal sector employment, may indicate the need for a different pattern of disbursement priorities in many SSA countries. Indeed, developmental needs in many SSA countries are likely to indicate that core finance for preemployment courses at training institutions, together with innovative methods of financing training for microenterprises and the informal sector, should be the first disbursement priority. Support for enterprise training may be given less weight than accorded in middle-level developing countries in other continents. Whatever the merits of such expenditures, pressures on public budgets may well result in the neglect of disadvantaged groups, unless designated funding is forthcoming from donors.

Training provision and disbursement: uneasy bedfellows

Tanzania. The Vocational Education and Training Authority (VETA) in Tanzania, in its triple role as national training provider, financier, and regulator, shows how the current pattern of disbursements is not conducive to achieving the wider goals (as set out in the 1994 Act establishing VETA) of a demand-driven, cost-effective national training system.

VETA grew out of the former National Vocational Training Division (NVTD) of the Ministry of Labor. Under the Act, the NVTD was given national responsibilities for all aspects of training. It is mainly financed by a 2 percent payroll levy, which has displaced government funding of public training provision, and by donor support. While VETA inherited the vocational training centers of the NVTD, continuing its role as public sector provider, it was also to preside over a new decentralized, regional structure (including regional boards) aimed at meeting the needs of local labor markets. This would include offering support to non-government training institutions on a competitive basis.

In practice, VETA's triple role as provider, financier, and overseer of the national training system has led to an internal conflict of interests in its activities. The VETA-owned, largely supply-driven training centers, providing mainly preemployment courses for the formal sector, dominate the activities of the regional structures; they receive the bulk of disbursements, which are not made on the basis of objective allocation criteria (see Chapter 8). In the budget for 2000, only about 5 percent of the recurrent budget (to be increased to 8.8 percent in 2001) is assigned to other, non-VETA-owned, training providers (under the category "VET provision support," which also covers informal sector training, disadvantaged groups, and, in principle, enterprise training). Thus, the same nominal budgetary allocation for VET support is made to each regional board, regardless of differing regional needs, and the transfer by regional boards of expenditures from other budget categories is disallowed.

Clearly, the protected status given by VETA to its own training centers is grossly distorting the training market by offering training at its centers at highly subsidized rates, making it difficult for private providers to compete. This prevents moves to open the field competitively to private providers and impedes the development of open, demand-driven, and low-cost regional training markets, which was a major objective of the 1994 reforms.

It will be apparent that the levy system as now operated in Tanzania is akin to the Latin American (revenue-raising) model, which is concerned primarily with funding public training institutions. In the VETA system, the bulk of levy proceeds are assigned to the funding of VETA-owned institutions; there are no elements of a levy-grant system for enterprises, though formally this is not ruled out by the Act. Yet, the Latin American model has been evolving over time. The model, in its pure form, has given way increasingly to a broader range of objectives, in which new activities of the fund compete for funding allocations with the traditional task of financing fund-owned training centers. In the case of VETA, these multiple objectives have been thrust upon a young institution, within which vested interests may have stunted the growth of these new, highly desirable developments.

The question arises whether, in the SSA context of "instant institutional development," the financing role of national training funds can be reconciled with responsibilities for training provision. While in the traditional Latin American model the training fund (or authority) was able to accommodate these evolving roles, the VETA experience may suggest that a separation of funding allocation from provision may be more appropriate in many SSA countries. But we must be careful not to rush to judgment on this issue. In an insightful contribution (discussed in Athumani and Ngowi 1999), Ssebuyoya (1997) comments on the difficulties that VETA is experiencing in its transition from a centralized government training department to an autonomous and decentralized authority with far broader responsibilities. Organizational change on this scale requires a new mind-set from staff. Yet, Ssebuyoya observes that while staff inherited from the former NVTD tended to resist change, new staff recruited from outside were more ready to "push new and fresh ideas into the VETA system." So, it is possible that this dichotomy may be transitional and resolved in the course of time.

Mauritius. Experience with the Industrial and Vocational Training Board (IVTB) in Mauritius provides another case in point. It too performs a triple role—in allocating training funds (financed by government and a payroll levy), in training provision at its own centers, and in regulating the training system. Bredie (1997) argues that "This is not an optimal situation ... and is bound to create conflicts of interest." The IVTB is unlikely to be encouraged to provide critical evaluation of its own training programs and, in some areas, subsidized public institutional training is crowding out private training provision. Bredie calls for a separation of the IVTB into two agencies, one responsible for providing training, the other for the wider regulatory activities, including administering the levy-grant system and disbursing training funds. Public training providers would need to compete for public funding on broadly equal terms with private training institutions—the proverbial "level playing field."

Zambia. In Zambia, potential conflict among the three functions of training regulation and coordination, of funding, and of training provision was avoided with the setting up of the Zambian training authority—the Technical Education, Vocational and Entrepreneurship Training Authority (TEVETA) in 1998. An autonomous body with a mandate to regulate and coordinate technical education, vocational, and entrepreneurship training provision in Zambia, it has no training provision or funding role. TEVETA is not a training fund nor does it own or operate any training centers. With the demise of the government Department of Technical Education and Vocational Training (DTEVT), out of which TEVETA was formed, the 23 DTEVT training centers ceased to be run publicly and funded from the public purse. The training centers are now placed under independent management boards and, according to present plans, over the long term will need to cover costs by generating revenues from training and other activities. In the interim, government will pay staff salaries (Haan 2001).

Governance, control, and stakeholder representation

Central issues in governance and control

Governance varies considerably across training funds; yet, the efficacy of a training fund may depend on the framework of governance and control within which it functions. Some training funds are part of broader, usually autonomous national training authorities, vested with a wide range of powers and responsibilities in the training field beyond those of financing; others are more narrowly focused funds, as discussed thus far in this chapter. There is a tendency for national training authorities to be more independent and autonomous than funds, but this is not always the case, and will depend on the legal and institutional framework. Most training funds are statutory, quasi-autonomous bodies; they usually operate under the general umbrella of labor ministries and, more immediately, of a board with some degree of stakeholder representation.

The issue of governance has important implications for the successful functioning of training funds. To understand why this is so, it is necessary to answer a basic question: Why is it necessary to establish separate training funds, rather than use a designated account earmarked for training within government (the treasury or the ministry of labor)? Historically, separate training funds were developed as part of training levy systems to protect the levy proceeds from government encroachment, an issue still relevant today. But the main raison d'être for training funds, as such, is not merely protective. Indeed, not all training funds derive income from levies.

The more positive reasons for establishing training funds may be demonstrated by an analogy with university funding organizations in place in many countries. These organizations serve as a buffer between government and the university system. Composed of university experts and public figures, the buffer organizations can evaluate and plan the needs of the university system as a whole and minimize political intervention in the allocation of funding. Analogously, management bodies of training funds can evaluate the needs and priorities of the training system as a whole (or at least that part for which it has a mandate), free from political influence. Disbursement policies and decisions are more likely to coincide with market needs since membership of fund management bodies is usually representative of the major stakeholders, including employers, unions, and trainers. Consensus building and partnership are thus facilitated, cementing ties for cooperation on wider training issues. These benefits of autonomy are unlikely to be forthcoming where ministerial control remains strong, where governing boards are advisory rather than managerial, and where they are not representative.

However, Herschbach (1990) notes that the level of government control (and the extent of board autonomy) is not necessarily linked with training fund effectiveness; the central issue is how, and for what purposes, control is used. He quotes the well-known Singapore case where the Vocational and Industrial Training Board, while strongly influenced by government, still functioned effectively to further national development goals, with training becoming a tool for the achievement of the government's policies for growth and employment. At the other extreme, government control may be detrimental. Often, training fund boards have been ineffective because government control has been used "to accomplish social and political rather than economic objectives, have diverted funds to nontraining purposes, or have exploited rather than assisted employers" (Herschbach 1990).

ZIMDEF

ZIMDEF, the veteran training fund in Zimbabwe, provides a striking case of governance shortcomings. Under the 1984 Act setting up ZIMDEF (amended in 1994), the relevant minister is given overriding powers as sole trustee of the fund. The minister appoints the chief executive (and fixes the terms and conditions of appointment), directs his activities, and approves the capital, revenue, and recurrent expenditure budgets. He is advised by the National Manpower Advisory Council, whose mandate covers all aspects of national manpower development, not just the fund, and its role is, indeed, purely advisory.

The fund was set up to finance apprenticeship training (apprentice wages for the first two years and direct training costs) and reimbursement to companies for approved training. For many years, the fund's activities have generated large annual surpluses because of declining numbers of apprentices and the relatively low level of total company reimbursement payments. The latter has resulted from a narrow definition of reimbursable training, which is restricted to professional courses at external institutions and virtually excludes continuing on-the-job training. It is also the result of complicated reimbursement procedures. ZIMDEF does not support training for the informal sector. With the transfer of ZIMDEF from the labor ministry to the new Ministry of Higher Education and Technology (MoHET) in 1988, a change in orientation became apparent. A "tripartite culture"—with a readiness to work with industry and a concern with labor market issues—was replaced by an educational focus.

A recent report on the fund, commissioned by the Confederation of Zimbabwe Industries, concluded that the centralization of the trusteeship of the Fund in MoHET "has resulted in inadequate capacity for the proper and effective direction and management of the fund" (Ndoro and Durango 2001). The authors could detect "no transparent medium-term and long-term strategic plan, which is based on the effective consultation and consensus of all stakeholders." Criteria and procedures for budget allocation were not apparent and prioritization was poor, with considerable diversification into noncore activities. Funds are used increasingly for broader purposes, such as university education and controversial investments in real estate.

The financial statements of the fund for 1999 show that as much as 20 percent of fund income was derived from nonlevy sources, mainly from interest on short-term investments from accumulated surpluses. The surplus for the year constituted 28 percent of total income (35 percent of proceeds from the levy). Less than 20 percent of training levy proceeds was used to support the apprenticeship scheme, while only some 12 percent was returned to companies as grants and rebates. In parallel, property assets tripled in 1999; the value of this increase exceeded the total of all disbursements for manpower development and training in that year.

Considerable disquiet about the operations of the fund is evident, with increasing calls for the establishment of an independent tripartite management board to oversee its operations.

Stakeholder representation

Most training funds are managed by a governing board, usually operating (with differing degrees of autonomy) under the umbrella of the Ministry of Labor. Board representation is usually tripartite (government, unions, and employers), frequently (as in the case of Côte d'Ivoire) divided equally between the three main stakeholders. On occasion, additional membership is drawn from public figures from the education and training sectors.

Often, the issue of board membership composition has been a cause of disagreement, especially where employers have argued for greater levels of representation. In those cases where company payroll levies provide a substantial part of training fund income, it might be both appropriate and politic that employers should feel they have some control on the uses to which the levies are put. Yet, employer representation varies widely from fund to fund. In Madagascar, 10 of the 12 members of the Board of Directors of the National Council for Technical and Vocation Training (CNFTP) are employer representatives, while in both Côte d'Ivoire (Managing Committee of the Vocational Training Development Fund [FDFP]) and Kenya (the advisory National Industrial Training Council), employer representatives constitute a third of the membership of these tripartite bodies. In Tanzania (VETA), only 2 out of 11 members of the management board are employer representatives.

But even where training levies are not the main or sole source of funding, a substantial employer presence on management boards may be desirable in order to forge links with employers generally, and as part of the process of fostering demand-related training. Employer members of training fund boards may be seen as representing the ultimate consumers of the outputs of the training system and, as such, may have relevant inputs to make in board decisionmaking. Yet, overall, there appears to be no strong link between the size of employer representation on training fund management boards and the effectiveness of training fund management. This is not surprising. The presence of a substantial representation of employers on a training fund board does not mean that its composition is *representative* of the broad constituency of employers; nor may the individuals be the most suitable for the tasks at hand. For example, as Herschbach (1990) notes: "the tendency is for larger, more politically adroit employers to be represented on Boards of Directors, and the interests of smaller employers may not be adequately addressed." He concludes that to function successfully, a number of elements must be present: a national training authority (and training fund board) "must be free of self-serving domination, by either government or private groups; it must truly represent the constituents that it serves, control its budget, and possess the autonomy to make policy and carry out decisions."

Sectoral funds

Sectoral (industry-based) training funds offer an alternative to the national (centralized) funding model discussed thus far. In some countries, sectoral training funds, based on training levies, have been introduced in one or two sectors only, particularly in the absence of a robust national training system to cater to the needs of a strong and growing economic sector (Franz 2000). These levies are often introduced by the industry in question. Franz (2000) discusses two SSA examples: construction in Botswana and the fishing industry in Namibia. The Botswana Construction Training Trust Fund is financed through a levy based on the value of tendered contracts; levy income, which in principle is matched by government subventions, is used mainly to finance a training center providing tailor-made courses for construction companies. In Namibia, a levy based on fish catch is used, in part, to finance a training center for the maritime professions.

Although examples of the genre are limited, national systems of sectoral funding are better known, notably the short-lived industrial training board system in the United Kingdom. Nationwide sectoral funds may be financed by a common, across-sector levy (as in South Africa since 1999) or the levy may differ by sector (as in Kenya), reflecting differing situations and needs in sectors.

A national system of sectoral funds offers the advantages of flexibility and the ability to focus more directly on the particular, often differing, sectoral training needs. Sectoral training funds may be more acceptable to employers because of a greater industry-specific orientation, less bureaucracy, and greater sense of "ownership." But the model has not been widely adopted. A system of sectoral funds, precisely because of its parochial focus, is unable to offer the broad, integrating approach to funding policy that was outlined above. It may produce a narrow approach to training, with duplication of efforts and a failure to develop a functional approach to common core skills, transferable across industries. It is poorly adapted to meeting regional needs. Moreover it is inflexible in not allowing for redistribution of funding across sectors nor for the financing of nonsector-related national skill priorities or other special training programs. Hegelheimer (1988), provides a scathing critique of sectoral funds (he refers to them as "branch" funds). He argues that they tend to result in narrow, sector-specific training; while discussed in the context of European experience, the issues raised are relevant to developing countries too.

The development of training funds in particular sectors might be appropriate in those settings where financing mechanisms are in their infancy and are being developed on a piecemeal basis. However, and especially within developing countries, a nationwide system of sector-based training funds has not, thus far, been seen as providing a suitable model for emulation. In this context, recent funding reforms in South Africa, to which we now turn, are of particular relevance in their attempt to develop a new national, sectoral-based funding system that preserves the benefits of sectoral funding while avoiding some of its major shortcomings. The progress of these reforms will be followed with much interest.

Sectoral funding in South Africa

The ITB system. South African industrial training boards (ITBs), recently transformed and broadened under current reforms into sector education training authorities (see below), constituted a unique feature of its training system. In terms of comparative international practice, the 27 ITBs were unusual in being sector-based and in being voluntary. These two central features have constituted built-in weaknesses to the system, militating against an effective system able to meet the needs of a changing economy. A major objective of the current reforms is to correct these deficiencies.

The voluntary nature of the ITB system led to low sectoral and labor force coverage, inefficient levy collection, and underfunding of formal sector training. Yet, the large number of sector-based training boards, combined with a lack of central steering of the national training system, resulted in considerable underprovision of skills development to meet social needs, particularly in relation to school-leavers, the unemployed, and rural populations. The system did not facilitate the shifting of resources between industries to meet the needs of emerging sectors. This is of particular concern to the South African economy, which is undergoing a process of considerable structural change, with major shifts in the composition of output and employment; these changes may be expected to intensify over time.

SETAs—new sectoral intermediaries. The 1998 Act provides for the introduction of tripartite sectoral agencies, or intermediaries, to promote high quality and relevant education and training provision at the sector level. These new SETAs are being developed from existing ITBs, whose functions have been broadened to include the development of sector skills plans that align to the national skills strategies and targets. SETA councils are tripartite, with an equal representation of employees and employers.

SETAs will be funded from the proceeds of a compulsory national skills development levy on enterprises (replacing the voluntary ITB levies, where in place), set at 1 percent of taxable employee remuneration (initially at 0.5 percent). Levies will be collected by the South African Revenue Services (although in specific cases, by the relevant SETA); 80 percent of sectoral levy income will be deposited in sectoral skills development funds to be managed by SETAs. These funds will be disbursed as grants to firms that meet accredited training criteria linked to the sector skills plan. The remaining 20 percent of revenues will be credited to the new National Skills Fund.

The national skills fund. The establishment of a national skills fund is an important step toward providing more structured and stable funding for a range of nonsector-related training activities. Levy income will be supplemented by government allocations and donor funds. The fund will finance national skills priorities, including employee training in priority sectors and skill categories, assistance to sectors in decline by facilitating restructuring, worker adult basic education programs, and the new system of "learnerships" (apprenticeships). It will also assist target groups, such as women, youth, the unemployed, people with disabilities, and rural communities. The earmarking of a fifth of levy income to the fund will provide it with a more stable resource base than would be forthcoming if it were forced to compete for funding in the budgetary process. But this funding will be at the expense of enterprises rather than the taxpayer—a bone of contention between business and government.

From training funds to national training authorities

Many national training funds are centrally concerned with the financing of training provision at the fund's training centers or operating a levy-grant scheme. In the latter case, training funds will need to monitor the training system to some extent; they may also provide a range of services for enterprises related to the functioning of the levy-grant system, including consulting with enterprises to help them develop and improve training capacity. In many countries, however, national training funds are "upgraded" to perform a far wider range of activities. Designated as

NTAs—though sometime retaining the designation "training fund"—these bodies are often charged with the central role of responsibility for national skills development.

To respond to the developing skill needs of the economy and to be able to act rather than just react in relation to technological and industrial change, public training systems need a greater degree of independence than is forthcoming from line ministries. NTAs will often play a central coordinating role in planning the national training system, in developing training policy, supervising national skills testing and certification, as well as providing necessary information services and developing appropriate labor market signals. Independence from close ministerial control and strong representation of employers on NTA management boards can provide the conditions for forging strong industrial links, flexibility and responsiveness, and for fostering private training institutional development. Atchoarena (1996) provides an insightful discussion of NTAs.

While NTAs may not necessarily be funded by training levies, the availability of stable funding may be an important ingredient for success. Equally important is the requirement that NTAs be vested with real authority; too often NTAs lack teeth and are essentially consultative to the relevant minister, rather than executive. In Ghana, attempts to set up a national overseer body for training led to the establishment in 1990 of the National Coordinating Committee for Technical and Vocational Education and Training (NACVET), a largely advisory body within the Ministry of Education and without separate legal status. In Kenya, the National Industrial Training Council is purely advisory, with little real impact; it has presided over an ongoing deterioration in public training provision (King 2001). Following some considerable controversy, the new National Skills Authority in South Africa (discussed below), too, has been allotted a purely advisory role.

National skills development coordination in South Africa

In the wide consultative process that led up to reform of the national training system in South Africa, broad agreement was reached on the need to introduce a mechanism to secure national coherence and strategic direction for the training system; the advisory status of the National

Training Board (NTB) had not provided scope for these activities. The discussion was moving strongly toward the creation of a new tripartite central coordinating body. Given the voluntaristic traditions in the South African training sector, this body would not exercise the strong degree of central control found in NTAs in many other countries. But it would be charged with assuming overall responsibility for developing national policy, national research capacity, monitoring and evaluation studies, coordinating the activities of sectoral training bodies (SETAs), and providing them with advice and support services.

However, the government's proposals for the governance of the national training system, as set out in the Green Paper, and later formalized in the new Act, are a far cry from this scenario. The NTB was restructured into a new tripartite National Skills Authority (NSA), but employers and labor are each represented by only 5 of the 25 voting members. While, according to the Green Paper, the NSA will be given "much stronger advisory powers than the old NTB," it will nevertheless remain purely advisory to the Minister of Labor. It appears that, under the new system, the Minister and the Department of Labour will assume more control over the governance of the national training system as a whole. And rather than running the important new Skills Development Planning Unit, the NSA would only have "access" to it; the unit will be based within the Department of Labour.

In sum, under these new arrangements, union and employer representatives have only an advisory role, thus denying the main stakeholders a strong role in the governance of the national training system. Instead, the ministerial role was strengthened. The opportunity was missed to create an independent, tripartite training authority to coordinate the national training system and assume control over training development and policy.

Training fund sustainability

An important objective of establishing national training funds (particularly when financed by company training levies) is to provide sustained and stable funding for the training programs they support. In practice this has not always been achieved, notably when funds do not receive the resources that have been designated to finance its activities; such an outcome not only compromises the raison d'être of the fund but may also call into question its sustainability over the long term. A shortfall of funding may arise for many reasons, but four are of particular note.

First, training levy proceeds, designated for the training fund, may be absorbed instead into general government revenues. This has occurred in a number of SSA countries, including The Gambia, Togo, and Côte d'Ivoire. In the latter case, after working well for two decades, the national training fund became insolvent and was liquidated in 1992 (Atchoarena 1996) because of the failure (occasioned by financial difficulties) of the Ministry of Finance to transfer training levy proceeds to the fund. The new institutional framework introduced in 1992 (including the establishment of a new training fund, the FDFP) provided for the direct transfer of levy income to a secure FDFP account.

In The Gambia and Togo, the payroll levy was collected by the Ministry of Finance but rarely, if ever, transferred to the fund. In the Togo case, the levy was one of the major income sources planned for the national training fund, which was never fully operational. There appear to be a number of reasons for this, including the country's continuing financial crisis. But it would also seem that the fiscal authorities (in Togo, as in many other countries) never fully endorsed the concept of earmarking levy revenues for training. Indeed, earmarked taxes are widely regarded as a departure from sound fiscal practice, it being argued that the government should reserve the right to allocate its revenues on an annual basis according to current realities and new priorities, rather than being constrained by prior commitments. Counter arguments, based on benefit grounds, can be marshaled in support of earmarked training taxes, but the case needs to be argued clearly and consensus reached prior to implementation.

A second reason for a shortfall of income to training funds is the failure of financing bodies to meet their funding obligations. This was a contributing cause to the inoperability of the Togo fund: the European Union failed to mobilize its expected initial, and substantial, contribution to the fund. Governments too may not make the required contributions to a training fund. While the introduction of payroll levies aimed at revenue generation may be a legitimate method of lowering government expenditures, the government may overrespond. Thus, in Tanzania, government funding for the new training authority, VETA, which was planned to cover capital expenditures (while recurrent expenditures were to be met from the payroll levy), virtually ceased after the first year of VETA's activity.

Third, where fund income is based on training levies, funding may fall short of planned levels because of technical difficulties with levy collection; this is a potentially serious problem in many SSA countries, and we deal with this issue in the next chapter.

Finally, there is the problem of training fund sustainability over the long term, in particular where training funds have been launched by donors and are funded, in the main, externally. What happens when donor financing ends? The demise of the Togo training fund was knelled with the closing of donor credit, which had been the fund's mainstay since its inception. We have noted that levy proceeds were not transferred to the national training fund; faced with severe budgetary constraints, civil service salaries and debt service were seen as having prior calls on public resources. This problem of fund sustainability will be endemic in many SSA country situations where public budgets are likely to be severely constrained over the medium term and where the time is not ripe for introducing training levies. In this situation, overgenerous external support for national training funds, without the planned, complementary development of domestic funding, will result ultimately in moribund training authorities and empty coffers.

Lessons for policy: identifying good practice

Desired objectives for training funds

We have noted the considerable heterogeneity in objectives and practice among national training funds. Yet, from our wide-ranging discussion in this chapter, particularly relating to recently established funds or those being reformed or redesigned, we attempt to bring together central elements of the desired objectives of training funds; these, in turn, help identify the common threads in training fund "good practice."

Ten major objectives are identified, largely reflecting the emerging consensus discussed above; these are summarized in Table 5.2. Objectives 7–9 are discussed more fully in Chapter 8; the tenth objective is treated more comprehensively in Chapter 9.

Limitations. For a number of reasons most SSA training funds, in practice, fall short of the standards listed in Table 5.2. Funds may suffer from deficient design, poor implementation, or malfunction; we discuss some SSA cases more fully below. But in other cases, the scope of the fund's responsibilities has been circumscribed purposefully; for example, the training fund in Tanzania is not concerned with enterprise training, while the Industrial Training Fund in Malawi (now replaced) was restricted to supporting the national apprenticeship scheme. Factors such as limitations in institutional development, implementation capacity, or funding sources may require the prioritization of efforts at the outset, subsequently moving into a broader range of operations. As noted above, current discussions for the establishment of a pilot national training fund in Zambia indicate the desirability of funding from government and donor sources initially, only moving slowly toward the introduction

Table 5.2 Ten Desired Objectives for National Training Funds

1. National Training Funds should constitute a mechanism for augmenting and pooling resources available for the financing of training provision and for disbursing these funds to training providers.
2. Fund income may be derived from various sources, alone or in combination, including earmarked training levies (usually imposed on enterprises), government budgets, donor allocations, and Fund-generated income.
3. The Fund should constitute a protected source of funding for training, ideally isolated from public sector budgetary vicissitudes and thus providing greater stability in training finance over the longer term.
4. Participation of the main stakeholders (especially employers) in Fund policy formation and management, through active membership of the Fund's governance institutions, has an important role to play in building consensus on training issues; this may be particularly important where enterprise training levies are in place.
5. Depending on the defined responsibilities of the Fund, support could be available for all major forms of training—pre-employment, initial and apprenticeship training, continuing training (on- and off-the-job) and training for special groups, including minorities, the disadvantaged, and the poor.
6. Funding allocation would take account of the needs of the training system as a whole and depend on agreed national priorities.
7. In principle, training finance would be allocated to all types of training providers, including public and private training institutions and enterprises providing training; ideally, attention also would be given to the special training needs of small micro enterprises and informal sector producers.
8. Allocations to public and private institutional providers would be made on a competitive basis, with the aim of raising institutional efficiency, integrating training markets and moving towards demand-driven provision.
9. These objectives would be furthered through parallel policies for the decentralization of control over public sector providers and greater institutional autonomy.
10. The Training Fund would take measures to encourage enterprises to invest more in worker training, including the use, as appropriate, of various financing mechanisms including levy-grant schemes, direct subsidies, and matching grants.

of a payroll levy and levy-grant system (in line with declared government policy) at a later stage. Preliminary discussions in Ethiopia are following similar lines.

Policy implementation

We have noted the diversity in practice among national training funds in SSA countries, especially in terms of the emerging consensus as outlined in Table 5.2. This is legitimate because training fund activity will need to reflect the range of objectives chosen, in turn influenced by the stage of institutional development, particular skill and human resource needs, and available funding sources (including the feasibility of imposing training levies). In rare cases, a country with more advanced training practice and mature administrative and institutional development may have moved on to a full-fledged national training authority—although this normally would not be apposite for SSA countries. Whatever the given objectives and coverage of the national training fund, however, successful outcomes are unlikely unless six key conditions are satisfied. These conditions are (a) security of income to the fund; (b) fund management autonomy and control; (c) stakeholder representation; (d) a restriction of fund activities to national training needs; (e) avoidance of the role of training provider; and (f) transparency of fund management decisionmaking. These conditions are outlined in Table 5.3.

Table 5.3 Key Conditions for Training Fund Success

Key condition	Justification
1. Security of Income	Assure adequate levels, stability, and sustainability of training fund incomes.
2. Autonomy & Control	Secure decisionmaking autonomy of management board and its control over budget allocations.
3. Stakeholder Ownership	Substantial representation of the major stakeholders on management board, engendering a sense of ownership—particularly of employer groups, where training levies are in place.
4. Activities (and Disbursements) for National Training Needs Only	Ensure that training fund policies and disbursements are targeted according to defined national training needs and that extraneous (non-training) activities are avoided.
5. Avoid Role of Training Provider	Training centers run (and financed) by a training fund tend to receive high subsidies and preferential treatment; this distorts training markets and militates against moves towards an open, competitive training system.
6. Decisionmaking Transparency	Decisionmaking to be open and, in particular, the basis for fund allocation to be known and understood.

Priority must be given to ensuring the fund's financial integrity. Almost by definition, the most essential ingredient for the successful operation of a training fund is security of income—that is, that fund income be adequate (in relation to the range of activities and operations expected of it) and relatively stable. We have noted that too often these conditions are not met. The problem may arise at two levels.

The first is at the level of the *source* of funding. Many funds are under-resourced because potential sources of income to the fund are too limited. While most funds rely on training levies, the income generated may be meager because the modern employment sector (on which the levy falls) is small or the collection system poor. Again, training levies may not be in place because they are at present unfeasible. In all these cases, the fund will need to be financed, entirely or in part, by government allocations or donor funding; yet, both of these are less stable or less secure funding sources, especially over the long term. And the generation of income from a newly instituted training levy or the fresh availability of donor funding may displace existing government funding.

Second, income may be insecure at the *point of transfer* to the fund, particularly where training levy proceeds remain with the treasury and are used for general budgetary expenditures rather than accruing to the training fund. Particular attention must be paid, in both fund institutional design and implementation, to the need to ensure adequate levels, stability, and sustainability of training fund income.

These key issues—not only income security but also fund autonomy and control, stakeholder ownership, and the focus of activities of the fund—should be considered comprehensively and in detail in the early stages of fund design and not in an ad hoc manner during implementation. Finally, the enabling legislation establishing the fund will have to incorporate clear directives to ensure that these conditions are secured.

Training funds in selected SSA countries: organization, funding source, and objectives

The chapter concludes with a summary presentation of the organizational structure, funding sources, and fund objectives in some 20 national training funds in SSA countries (Table 5.4, following page).

Table 5.4 Training Funds in Selected SSA Countries: Organization, Funding Source and Fund Objectives

Country	Organization (year established)	Funding source	Objectives (and sectors covered)	Comments on the working of the scheme
Angola (planned)	National Vocational Training Agency (INAFOP). Planned—Employment and Training Fund		Placement of unemployed. Improving worker productivity through in-company training. Aimed at modern sector	
Benin	Planned project to put into action the National Vocational Training Policy adopted in 1998 Training fund to be established	2/3 IDA,1/3 Government	To provide training for 25,000 workers. Modern, informal, agricultural and unemployed	
Cape Verde	Training support fund (TSF), overseen by Executive Committee and administered by Project Coordination Unit (PCU)	World Bank and Government	Development of market-oriented training courses. Training institutions and enterprises	
Côte d'Ivoire	Fonds de Devellopement de la Formation Professionelle (1991), an amalgamation of the Apprenticeship Fund (1959) and the Continuing Vocational Training Fund (1977)	Apprenticeship tax (0.4% payroll) Continuing vocational training tax (net—1.2% payroll). Donor funding	Apprenticeship training and continuing in-service training. Support of training programs for the informal sector (sectoral cross-subsidization)	Problem of non-transfer of levy proceeds by the Treasury to the Fund (particularly in early 1990s) largely solved by establishment of special fund account
Djibouti	Planned—National Council for Training and Employment (CNFE). Never operational.			

(Continued)

Table 5.4 *(continued)*

Country	Organization (year established)	Funding source	Objectives (and sectors covered)	Comments on the working of the scheme
Gambia, The	National Council for Technical Education and Vocational Training			Levy assessed on firms but collected and deposited in Treasury—never used for training
Kenya	Industrial Training Levy Fund (1997)	Sectoral training levies (not payroll based)	Mainly formal sector: indentured learnerships and apprenticeships, skills upgrading and management courses	Levy collection and fund administration by the Directorate of Industrial Training. Fall in numbers of apprentices overtime. Poor quality of public sector training (National Vocational Training Center at Nairobi)
Lesotho	Tripartite structure to oversee establishment of national guidelines and TVET reform			
Madagascar	National Council of Technical and Vocational Education and Training, CNFTP. Manages Fund of Intervention for Vocational Training (FIFP).	IDA and State		Payroll levy planned for future implementation. Regional and sub-regional training boards
Malawi (to be replaced)	Industrial Training Fund (1973)	Differential head tax (on skilled workers), by skill category, in Government and private sector	Finance of national apprenticeship scheme reimbursement of apprenticeship wage and grants to technical colleges providing formal courses	If tax shifted onto skilled workers, latter finance the costs of training apprentices

Mali	Fond d'Appui a la Formation Professionnelle et de l'Apprentissage (FAFPA)	0.5% I payroll levy	Fund to develop demand-driven employer-financed skills upgrading and apprenticeship training. Formal (public domain); Informal (private domain)	Fund finances 75–90% of initial training costs, depending on age of trainees
Mauritania	Institutional Support Fund (ISF) Training Support Fund (TSF)	ISF financed by FAC TSF financed by IDA	ISF—to fund quality improvements developed by training institutions; TSF to finance initiated by micro enterprises TSF—for training needs of entrepreneurs and small businesses mainly in the informal sector	
Mauritius	Industrial Vocational Training Board—IVTB (1988)	1% payroll levy. Government	IVTB training centers focus on pre-employment training. Levy-grant scheme directed to in-service training	
Nigeria	Industrial Training Fund (ITF): Governing Council fulfils role of national training authority: Industrial and Vocational Training Board	1% payroll levy plus annual budget from ?????	Promoting employer-based training via levy reimbursement (up to about 60% of levy contribution). Some course provision at ITF training centers. Formal sector	

(Continued)

Table 5.4 *(continued)*

Country	Organization (year established)	Funding source	Objectives (and sectors covered)	Comments on the working of the scheme
Senegal	National Agency for Vocational Training—ONFP (1988)	5 percent of the Fixed Contribution (employer tax of 3% of gross salaries). State grants	Formal sector training	Fully-fledged Fund is envisaged in the PDEF (Plan Decennal de l'Education et de la Formation)
South Africa	National Skills Fund (1999)	A fifth of the proceeds of a 1% payroll levy. Government contribution planned. 80% of levy proceeds finance sectoral training funds	To meet natioanl strategic objectives, especially long-term unemployed and other targeted special-needs groups and sectors	Fund largely controlled by the Treasury.
Tanzania	Vocational Education and Training Authority (VETA)	2% payroll levy	Finance of formal (mainly VETA-owned) training institutions	Regional training boards
Togo	National Training Fund (NTF)	Donors, government	Fund available for projects in the public, private and informal sectors	Payroll levy remains in the Treasury
Zambia	Technical Education, Vocational and Entrepreneurship Authority (TEVETA)	2% (suggested)		Payroll levy planned for future implementation
Zaire	A national training agency	Earmarked payroll tax		
Zimbabwe	Zimbabwe Manpower Development Fund (ZIMDEF) and also Vocational Training Fund (VTF)	1% payroll levy on private and parastatal companies	Finance of apprenticeship and other approved, mainly professional, formal sector training	Leakage to other uses: tertiary education, real estate etc. Payroll levy collected by ZIMDEF

Note: There are training funds also in: Cameroon, CEA, Chad, the Congo and Gabone.

Note

1 A somewhat dated, though still highly relevant, discussion of national training agencies (and funds) is given in Herschbach (1990).

CHAPTER 6

Training Levies

Earmarked levies on enterprise payrolls have become the most widely adopted funding mechanism for financing training, both in public training institutions (usually under the aegis of a national training authority) and in enterprises. They are already central to training finance policies in many SSA countries, and a number of other countries are examining the benefits and feasibility of introducing payroll levies to finance training. Given the centrality of payroll levies in any consideration of training finance, this chapter details the types, purposes, pros and cons, and efficacy of payroll taxes. Chapters 7 and 9 continue the discussion.

Alternative training levy schemes

While payroll levies are the best-known and most widespread form of training taxation, some countries (within SSA and beyond) have preferred other forms of training taxes. These training taxes, not based on payrolls, tend either to be sector-specific or are introduced to finance a narrow training outcome. The training tax in Malawi, now being replaced by a tax on payrolls, provides an example of the latter—a per capita tax levied on the employers of skilled workers in government and the private sector that is used to finance the national apprenticeship scheme. Examples of sector-level training taxes in SSA are more readily found; to these we now turn.

SSA sector levies

As examples of sector-based levies, we have already referred to training taxes in Botswana (in the construction sector, based on value of contracts) and in Namibia (a levy based on fish catch, in the fishing industry).

Mauritius. Legislation in Mauritius provides for the collection of a one-off, lump-sum levy on each bedroom in newly constructed hotels. The rationale for this levy is that new hotels utilize skills acquired through on-the-job training at existing hotels. This construction levy would be effective payment for this if invested in additional training. To date, however, this levy has not been collected.

Kenya. The best known scheme of this type is the Kenyan one—a national training tax system organized on the basis of 11 industry levy committees with differently based training taxes, none based on payrolls. Of the 11 industrial levy committees, 8 of them tax companies on the basis of a fixed sum per worker; in both building and construction and in saw-milling the levy is set at 0.25 percent of quarterly turnover, while the plantations output levy is based on the metric ton. In addition, the hotel and catering levy is fixed at 2 percent of total net takings of hotels and restaurants.

South Africa. Under the system of separate industrial training levies in South Africa (now replaced by a standard national payroll levy), industrial training boards were equally divided between those utilizing a tax system based on enterprise payrolls and on the number of workers employed. A minority of boards levied training taxes on some other basis. In sugar milling and refining, the levy was based on output ("sugar in tons"), while the Maritime Industry Training Board was about to introduce a levy linked to turnover (replacing income on a donation basis), in the form of a "training levy stamp" for each bill of entry submitted to customs (Republic of South Africa 1995).

SSA sector-based schemes have met with varying levels of success and, clearly, their main advantage is that they offer a means of tailoring the levy format to the specific characteristics and needs of the sector. Yet, the disadvantages of sectoral levies—and funds—remain, particularly their narrow focus obviating an integrated, national approach to the finance and planning of skills development. Thus, most countries have preferred to employ standard, national-level levy schemes, based on enterprise payrolls. The rest of this chapter will be concerned with national payroll levies.

Payroll levies: revenue generation

We have noted the usual division of national payroll tax schemes into two distinct groups, reflecting different underlying objectives: revenue-generation schemes (where levy proceeds are used to finance training provided by public sector institutions) and levy-grant schemes (aimed at encouraging training investment by firms themselves). This traditional dichotomy is becoming outdated, however, as evolving levy schemes take on a broader range of tasks, particularly in the context of the development of national training funds and training authorities. Although many schemes both finance public sector institutions and offer incentives for enterprise training, this distinction remains a useful analytical device. There are some cases of dual-objective, mixed schemes; but for most schemes, the main thrust is in one of these two directions.

In levy schemes aimed at revenue generation, levy proceeds are used mainly to support public sector training provision, with the emphasis on initial training at formal public training institutions. The levy scheme supporting VETA in Tanzania is of this type. The bulk of funding goes toward the finance of VETA public training centers; financial support is also provided for the national trades testing system.

In the SSA context especially, payroll levy schemes of this type may be seen as a mechanism for greater funding diversification, lightening the burden of training funding falling on the state. The expectation is that levy income would complement existing government financing, thus providing an additional source of funding, although this has not always been the case in practice (see Chapter 7 for a discussion of the Tanzanian experience). But there are also notable cases of the opposite tendency (as in The Gambia, for example), where "earmarked" training taxes are not used for financing public training but instead are absorbed into general government revenues (we discuss this phenomenon in more detail below). In addition to generating more funding for training, these kinds of levies offer a more stable form of funding than do government allocations.

Levy-grant schemes

Unlike revenue-generation schemes aimed at financing training institutions mainly in the public sector, levy-grant schemes focus on company in-service training. They create incentives for a firm to invest in the skills development of its work force, be it in the sphere of training on the job (setting up or extending and improving existing company training) or by sending workers to train externally. As noted in Chapter 3, the need for government intervention, via the introduction of levy-grant arrangements, arises because of shortcomings in the amount or quality of enterprise training. While there are numerous variants, Gasskov's three-fold classification of various types of levy-grant schemes has been widely adopted, and is presented here. Gasskov (1994) distinguishes between schemes concerned with cost reimbursement, cost redistribution (for which he employs the more general term "'levy-grant"), and levy exemption.

Cost reimbursement

Under this category of scheme, the training fund pays grants to firms on a cost-incurred basis for designated forms of training (both on and off the job). The purpose of these schemes is often misunderstood, particularly among employers. The scheme aims not at reimbursement of the levy as such, but rather reimbursement of training expenditures incurred (to encourage firms to train more or better). Thus, a training expenditure reimbursement ceiling is usually set, up to a given percentage of the levy paid. Firms that train to acceptable standards will receive back part of the levy paid as grants; nontraining firms are penalized by loss of the levy. In theory, the scheme usually could provide for full reimbursement of the levy contribution (particularly where a large number of firms do not train and claim). In practice, reimbursement is set below the value of the levy paid. This is because central administration costs must be covered and, particularly when run by a national training authority, there may be additional central expenditures on other training services.

Nigeria. The payroll levy serving the Nigerian Industrial Training Fund provides an example of a long-standing cost-reimbursement scheme. In addition to running the reimbursement scheme, the fund finances and operates a number of its own training centers, and its staff provide regular assistance to firms in identifying training needs and developing training plans (Gasskov 1994). Because of these other calls on levy income, plus the cost of supporting the fund's large bureaucracy, firms generally can qualify for cost reimbursements of not more than 60 percent of the levy paid; in practice, less than 15 percent of firms request training cost reimbursement.

Cost redistribution

This variant differs from cost reimbursement in that it aims at redistributing the burden of training expenditures among enterprises. Designed in particular to deal with the ill-effects that poaching by nontraining firms has on training supply (see Chapter 3), the mechanism redistributes levy funds away from companies that do not train, toward those that do. Since the emphasis is on the redistribution of cost burdens, training companies may receive grants far in excess of the amount of levy paid, thus providing strong incentives for firms to train. Such cost redistribution schemes are most strong where the bulk of levy proceeds is redistributed back to firms as grants and not used for other (albeit training) purposes.

The classic example of this redistribution mechanism is the faulted system of industrial training board levies in the United Kingdom—and particularly that of the largest of the boards, in the engineering industry. In the latter case, the training levy was set at a rate (2.5 percent of payroll) sufficiently high to result in total levy proceeds approximating total annual training investments by all firms in the industry. This sum was then distributed back to training firms only, according to formulae designed to measure company training efforts (Ziderman 1978).

Mauritius. There seem to be no clear examples of cost-redistribution schemes in SSA. The case of the levy-grant system in Mauritius is instructive because it contains elements of cost redistribution, in the sense that firms may in principle receive back, in grants, up to 200 percent of levy payments. However, it is not a cost-redistribution scheme because about half of levy income is assigned to support institutional training in public training centers. While the incentive scheme overall (a combination of levy-grants and company tax concessions—see Chapter 9) allows reimbursement of up to 75 percent of training expenditures, uptake has not been high, though more recently it has been rising. In the early 1990s, about 20 percent of total levy proceeds were claimed and approved for refund; this level rose to about a third by the end of the decade.

Levy exemption

Arrangements for levy exemption are usually part of broader cost-reimbursement schemes, whereby firms adequately meeting their training needs are allowed to withdraw from the levy-grant system or at least to benefit from reduced levy assessments in proportion to their recognized training investments. A major advantage is that firms are freed from the bureaucratic fatigues of levy payment, and grant claim and potential cash-flow problems are avoided. While much discussed, this mechanism is found more typically in certain industrial economies rather than in developing countries. This mechanism seems to be lacking in SSA countries; an exception is the Côte d'Ivoire scheme.

Côte d'Ivoire. The Continuing Vocational Training (CVT) tax is the main revenue source for the national training fund (*Fonds de Développement de la Formation Professionnelle* [the Fund]) in Côte d'Ivoire. Under the CVT tax, firms are required to pay 1.2 percent of payroll (in addition, there is an apprenticeship tax of 0.4 percent of payroll). Firms may receive tax exemption of half their CVT tax obligations (0.6 percent) on submission, and Fund preapproval, of a company training plan (including training within and outside the firm), utilizing retained payroll tax obligations. Subsequently, the Fund monitors company training activity in accordance with the training plan; unused amounts are returned to the Fund. There is an additional incentive element built into the CVT system. Firms have the possibility of retaining up to an additional 50 percent of exempted payroll tax payments (0.9 percent of payroll instead of 0.6 percent). To do so, they must submit and implement training plans for three years and justify training expenditures beyond 1.6 percent of payroll; only a small percentage of firms avail themselves of this possibility.

Table 6.1 National Training Tax Schemes, Selected SSA Countries

Revenue Generation			Levy-Grant Scheme		
Country	Training tax	Used for training?	Country	Training tax	Used for training?
Gambia, The	?	No	Benin	2% of payroll	No
Mali	0.5% of payroll	Yes	Côte d'Ivoire	1.2% of payroll	Yes
Mauritius	1% of payroll	Yes	Kenya	Sectoral taxes (not based on payrolls)	Yes
Senegal	3% payroll	Very little			
Tanzania	2% of payroll	Yes	Nigeria	1.25% of payroll	Yes
Zaire	1% of payroll	Yes	Malawi	Based on number of skilled workers—being replaced by payroll levy	Yes
Zambia (planned)	2% of payroll (suggested)				
			South Africa	1% of payroll	Yes
			Togo	1% of payroll	No
			Zimbabwe	1% of payroll	Yes

Payroll levies in SSA

Table 6.1 presents information on SSA countries that operate a training tax regime of national scope. It will be seen that all current cases listed, with the exception of the Kenyan scheme, are payroll levy schemes; the favored levy rate is 1 percent of payroll. While the table assigns countries into one of the two major training tax scheme categories—revenue generation and levy-grant—it should be noted that many of the schemes, particularly levy-grant schemes, are in fact mixed ones.

Under schemes included in the revenue-generation category, the Tanzanian scheme is a pure revenue-generation scheme with no allowances (at least at this stage) for levy-grant arrangements. The Mauritius scheme, however, is clearly mixed. While some 50 percent of levy proceeds has traditionally been assigned to support public training institutions, about a quarter has been reimbursed back to firms, a proportion that has been rising more recently to about 40 percent.

Most levy-grants schemes contain elements of revenue generation. Nigeria is the clearest case of dual objectives (as noted above). The National Training Fund, established in 1971, is funded mainly by a 1 percent payroll levy, with additional financial support from federal government budgets (which was not forthcoming during the first decade, following its first year of operation). While the central activity of the fund is encouraging companies to invest in the skills development of their employees by offering training grants, in 1979 it opened its first vocational training center. Although on a much smaller scale than its levy-grant activities, the fund has continued to expand its direct training activities.

The levy-grant schemes in Kenya, Côte d'Ivoire, and South Africa all display elements of revenue-generation activities.

The Kenyan training levy-grant system is essentially aimed at financing the in-service training of workers in the industries covered. While no detailed information on the pattern of grant disbursements is published, a special exercise to identify disbursements by main expenditure category was carried out for the author in the early 1990s. This showed that some 85 percent of disbursements went as direct rebates to companies for training expenses (apprenticeship, management, and overseas courses), or indirectly in the form of fee payment to training institutions (industrial training centers and national polytechnics) for courses attended by company workers. Some 15 percent of expenditures were allocated for financing training-related matters more generally, departing from the concept of rebates. These items, normally paid out of public revenues, included the running of national seminars, fee payment, and expenses of trades test examiners as well as remuneration of instructors at industrial training center skill upgrading courses leading to trade tests.

In both the Côte d'Ivoire and South African schemes, part of levy income is designated for the financing of national training activities that are usually regarded as the government's concern. In Côte d'Ivoire, some 30 percent of CVT tax proceeds (net of tax obligations retained by firms) has been assigned for financing training proposals submitted by nongovernmental organizations (NGOs), local communities, and informal sector groups. Recently, levy funds allocated to training for the informal sector has risen to some 20 percent of fund allocations for training (Johanson 2001). The cross-subsidization of informal sector training by levy funds raised from formal sector enterprises is unusual, but is matched in provisions in the new levy-grant arrangements in South Africa.

As noted above, in South Africa 20 percent of the revenues from the new skills development levies on companies will be credited to the new National Skills Fund for across-sector strategic training initiatives and for the training of disadvantaged groups, activities that are generally funded from central government budgets.

Rationale: the benefit principle

Neither public finance experts nor treasury officials are enamored of earmarked taxes (for training or otherwise); they constrain the freedom of public officials to allocate public revenues on an annual, ad hoc basis according to current priorities. And many companies, claiming to see little benefit coming their way from a payroll levy scheme, point to the levy as constituting "just another tax."

There is now a sizable literature (beyond the scope of this paper) that attempts to identify the essential nature of payroll levies and to seek a theoretical justification for their imposition. One rationale for payroll levies, which has been widely quoted though not necessarily accepted, sees payroll taxation as a form of "reverse social security" (Whalley and Ziderman 1990). Based mainly on empirical literature from developed countries, it is argued that at least part of the incidence of a payroll levy is shifted onto workers in the form of lower wages. It is in this sense that a payroll levy scheme, earmarked for training, may be regarded as equivalent to a reverse social security scheme: The worker receives benefits in the form of training on entry into the labor market (or during the earlier years), and contributions are made subsequently over the working life. The relevance of this approach, even if broadly accepted, will depend on how far individual tax "payments" match the training benefits received. This in turn will depend on how equitably training opportunities are spread among workers, which, of course, will differ from case to case.

At a more pragmatic level, there probably would be wide agreement on the following proposition: Most payroll levy schemes, whether revenue generating or levy-grant, are used to finance training that is relevant (directly or indirectly) to the needs of the companies that pay the levy. In levy-grant schemes, enterprises may claim back part of training costs incurred, while in countries where enterprise training is weak or undeveloped, levies are used to finance public training institutions that provide skills for the formal sector. In this sense, training levy schemes may be regarded loosely as examples of benefit taxation, where taxpaying individuals or institutions are major beneficiaries of the uses to which the taxes are put.

Perhaps the most quoted, non-training-related, argument against the imposition of payroll levies is that, in raising the price of labor, they lead to a substitution toward more capital-using production methods and to lower employment. It is unlikely that this argument bears any weight in practice. Even where there is no tax shifting onto workers in terms of lower relative wages, a small addition to labor costs (usually only of 1 percent) is unlikely to affect wage employment significantly, except on the margin.

Coverage

Coverage of payroll levy schemes varies considerably from country to country, both in terms of sectoral coverage and size of firm included in the scheme. Most schemes exclude the public sector (in Mauritius and Tanzania, for example), which results in a cross-subsidization of training for public sector employees by the private sector, to the extent that levies finance public training institutions. In South Africa, central and provincial government remain outside the purview of the training levy legislation, but government departments are required to budget 1 percent of personnel costs for skills development.

Size of company included in the scheme also varies. Most schemes define eligibility in terms of firm size. While the Nigerian scheme includes enterprises with 25 workers or more, most schemes seem to be more comprehensive. All enterprises are covered in the Mauritius and South African schemes, while those in Kenya and Tanzania include all employers with four or more workers. Unusually, inclusion in the scheme in Zimbabwe is defined in terms of the size of the firm's annual wage bill (20,000 Zimbabwe dollars or over); given a monthly minimum wage of 5,000 dollars, this implies that coverage is comprehensive here too.

The efficacy of such broad coverage in many SSA country schemes is questionable. In practice, the bulk of revenue is collected from the minority of large and medium-sized firms. The relatively large number of microenterprises, the blurred definition of the informal sector, and the difficulties of small firm identification, registration, and levy collection all combine to produce considerable noncompliance in many countries. Legislation provides for fines or imprisonment for nonpayment in most countries; but these measures are either generally not employed (as was the case in Tanzania until the reversal in policy in this regard, introduced in

2001) or not applied to very small firms. The reason is clear: In many cases it is simply not cost-effective to follow up on small firms through litigation or even through dispatching inspector/collectors. Zimbabwe provides a case in point. Levy income from the smallest firms covered by the levy—usually family businesses—is minimal. Levy income lost from noncompliance of a very small firm may be only about 600 Zimbabwe dollars (about US$12), a sum hardly justifying the costs of collection follow-up. But considerable noncompliance brings the law (and the levy scheme) into disrepute and sends negative signals to complying firms about levy payment. A strong case can be made for raising the minimum firm size for inclusion in payroll levy schemes in SSA countries.

In many other regions, small firms are granted exclusion from training levy schemes. The main reason for this is not only that inclusion may not be practical (in terms of levy collection) but also that it may not be justified, particularly in levy-grant schemes. The administrative costs of applying for grants may be disproportionately high for small firms. Moreover, the training needs of very small firms differ from those of larger firms, in terms of expenditures (in relation to operating costs) and type of training. Much of the training for which rebates may be obtained in current SSA schemes is not relevant to very small firms (see Chapter 9).

Increasingly, various SSA countries are establishing financing schemes (Kenya and Ghana, for example) to deal with the needs of microenterprises and informal sector firms; but these tend to be based on subsidy (usually from government and donors) rather than on levy-grant approaches (Chapter 10). In Mauritius, however, a voucher scheme aimed at small firms has been introduced as part of the levy-grant system. The training voucher for small businesses would allow such enterprises to recoup some of their levy contributions in an accessible way.

Levy income generation

Alternative approaches to levy collection

The coverage of a levy scheme, in terms of sectors included and eligible firm size, will affect the amounts of levy income generated and, in turn, the amount of training activities it can finance. However, of far greater importance in defining the size of levy proceeds, given the defined coverage of the scheme, is the method of levy collection. Ineffective collection methods may result in considerable losses in potential levy income. While the literature gives much attention to the issue of the alternative uses of levy proceeds and distribution mechanisms, there has been little focus on the issue of levy income generation. The essential policy question we probe here is: Who should be charged with levy collection? Should the levy scheme itself take on this role or should this task be assigned to a collection agency, usually a branch of government? Before proceeding to a discussion of the pros and cons of these approaches, what may be learned from SSA county experience with levy collection?

Levy collection in SSA countries

The issues may best be viewed by examining current collection systems in selected SSA countries. Table 6.2 is divided into three blocks. The first two blocks relate to the use of a collection agency within general government tax-generation mechanisms (Côte d'Ivoire, South Africa, and Togo), or specialized agencies already involved in tax collection from companies on the basis of payroll (Mauritius and Tanzania). The third block contains examples of levy funds that collect their own levies; to this we now turn.

Self-collection. From the outset, many of the veteran levy-grant systems assumed responsibility for levy collection, including in Kenya, Zimbabwe, and Nigeria.

In Kenya, the Directorate of Industrial Training (DIT)—part of the Ministry of Labour—is the implementing agency for the levy-grant scheme. It is responsible for levy collection for the training fund (in reality, 11 separate sectoral training funds) as well as administering the levy-grant scheme as a whole, with the tripartite National Industrial Training Council acting in an advisory capacity to the DIT. The DIT is officially the sole national agency responsible for training; it performs a wide range of national training functions—including running its own training centers and the national trades testing system—in addition to levy collection. Thus, the DIT may be overextended. Moreover, these functions of the DIT are highly centralized; apart from the benefits this would offer in other areas, decentralization would be useful for identifying potential levy contributors

Table 6.2 Levy Collection Systems: Selected SSA Countries

Country	Collection Agency	Collection Fee (% of levy proceeds)	Initial Disposition of Levy Proceeds
Côte d'Ivoire	Tax Department, Finance Ministry	?	Previously deposited in a Treasury account; now levy proceeds transferred directly to outside training fund account
South Africa	South African Revenue Service	—	SARS 2% SARS pays levy proceeds into National Revenue Fund. Minister of Labour allocates proceeds between the National Skills Fund (20%) and sectoral training bodies (SETAs—80%)
Togo	Ministry of Finance	—	Absorbed into government revenues; not transferred to training fund
Mauritius	National Pension Board	4%	Transferred to training fund
Tanzania	National Social Security Fund (soon to be replaced by the Tax Revenue Authority)	7.5% (previously 5%)	Transferred to training fund
Kenya	Self collection (Department of Industrial Training)	—	Direct to training fund administered by the Department of Industrial Training, Ministry of Labour
Nigeria	Self collection	—	Direct to training fund
Zimbabwe	Self collection	—	Direct to training fund

and for ensuring that more contributions flowed into the fund (Ferej 1997).

The limited company coverage of the Nigerian scheme (restricted to firms with 25 or more workers) should be expected to ease the levy collection process. In practice, however, it appears that collection of the training levy imposes a heavy administrative burden on the Industrial Training Fund. Thus, in referring to the relatively large fund staff (1,450 staff to service 3,640 registered firms), B. C. Mhono notes: "the day-to-day struggle to raise levies from defaulting employers through such measures as reviewing firms' accounts, annual visits to firms, and consultancies" (in Gasskov 1994). The large geographical area covered does require a large area network of fund officers (some 850 employees) to deliver training services, as well as collect the levy from defaulting firms (only about half of registered firms are up to date with payments). The question remains whether levy collection, in this case and in others, would be more effective if assigned to a collection agency.

Agency collection. We first consider schemes that have utilized the services of general tax collection agencies. The experience here has been mixed. The major problem has been to ensure that levy proceeds are transferred to the training fund, particularly in periods of economic difficulty and tight government budgets. In the case of Togo and Côte d'Ivoire (from 1989 until the reforms instituted in 1992), as well as in Benin and The Gambia (see Table 6.1), levy funds were not transferred to the respective training funds but absorbed into general government revenues. With the restructuring of the training fund in Côte d'Ivoire in 1992, levy proceeds have been secure; they are now deposited directly to the fund rather than to a fund account in the treasury. Tanzania is moving toward levy collection by the Tax Revenue Authority (see below).

However, the new levy system now being introduced in South Africa also uses the tax system (South African Revenue Service—SARS) as the collection agency, with levy proceeds being deposited initially in the Treasury (National Revenue Fund [NRF]). The Minister of Labour then instructs the NRF to distribute 20 percent of the levy proceeds to the new National Skills Fund and 80 percent to the SETA responsible for training in each sector. Levy proceeds from companies not attached to a SETA are assigned wholly to the National Skills Fund. In theory, the use of the NRF as a depository might render levy proceeds less secure in periods of pressure on public budgets. The reform does allow for the possibility of individual SETAs collecting the levy from firms in their sector (and passing on 20 percent to the National Skills Fund); this would remove the possibility of central leakage of levy income to nontraining uses. Thus far, however, levy collection has not been delegated to any SETA.

In many ways, the use of a government department, already charged with the collection of a levy based on payroll, would appear to be the most effective collection method. But, again, experience is mixed. In Mauritius, the collection of the payroll levy appears to be extremely efficient. The levy is collected monthly by the National Pension Board, on behalf of the fund, as an add-on to the larger national pension insurance contribution.

The simplicity of this system, and the high incentives to report nonpayment of pension contributions, ensures a high rate of compliance (estimated at 96 percent). Experience in Tanzania is less positive, particularly in terms of levy compliance.

The debate in Tanzania—agency versus self-collection. The National Social Security Fund (NSSF) has acted as the levy-collection agency for VETA, the Tanzanian training authority, since the establishment of the levy scheme in 1995 (falling on all companies of four or more workers). It is widely believed that the NSSF performance has been substandard; this view has been a catalyst for calls within VETA to rescind the agency arrangement and to establish its own levy-collection unit. A brief review of this local debate may prove useful in highlighting some of the wider, general issues surrounding the advantages of self-collection and the use of a collection agent. In a recent VETA internal report arguing for the establishment of a levy-collection mechanism within VETA (VETA 2000), the main thrust of the argument against the NSSF is twofold: that it has not proved effective as a collection agency and that VETA could do the job cheaper. But neither argument has been proved.

The report claims that the NSSF gives second priority to training levy collection, which is not its central concern. In theory, this should not arise since the NSSF, in collecting the NSSF contribution, will contact employers also eligible for the training tax; however, NSSF inspectors are not always knowledgeable about the workings of the levy and may not be persuasive in eliciting payment from recalcitrant firms. The NSSF now receives a commission of 7.5 percent on all collections, representing a ministerial-imposed compromise between the 15 percent claim advanced by the NSSF (later reduced to 10 percent) and the former rate of 5 percent. So the NSSF may be a less-than-willing partner here. NSSF proceeds from its 20 percent levy on wages (comprising employer and worker contributions) are in the order of 70 billion shillings. Pro rata, the 2 percent training levy would result in 7 billion shillings (or somewhat less, because payment to the NSSF falls on all employers) and not the 5.2 billion shillings actually collected.

The report refers to an employer compliance rate of 20 percent and to collection of only 22 percent of potential levy proceeds, estimates far short of NSSF claims. However, while the report's estimates may be formally correct, they do not provide a full picture of the situation, since only about 28 percent of employers have registered for levy payment. In terms of registered employers, almost 70 percent of employers comply with levy payment, producing some 88 percent of potential proceeds. On the face of it, this seems to produce a better outcome than levy self-collection in Zimbabwe, where only 60 percent of registered companies pay the levy (of which 10 percent are in arrears).

The problem in Tanzania then is essentially one of low registration; this may reflect inefficiencies of the NSSF collection mechanism or may be the consequence of insufficient incentives in the form of a commission rate that is far below that which the NSSF claims is reasonable. Yet, lower agency fees are charged in Mauritius and South Africa (Table 6.2).

The question arises: Could VETA do the job cheaper—and better—than the NSSF? The report presents an internal (and therefore perhaps optimistic) exercise that estimates a self-collection cost of only about 27 percent of the projected agency fee (about 2 percent of proceeds). However, VETA's national board, reversing initial approval, rejected the proposal for self-collection. Arguments against the proposal include the risk that the core activity of VETA may be neglected as the administrative weight of levy collection diffuses attention away from training, and that the VETA regional offices lack the administrative capacity to undertake collection.

Finally, one advantage of self-collection in levy-grant schemes (as in Zimbabwe) is that collection inspectors also double up as "PR officers," and can play an important role in explaining the rebate system and encouraging firms to apply. This issue is not applicable for the Tanzanian revenue-generation scheme.

The debate has now been overridden by a unilateral decision of the Ministry of Finance to give the Tax Revenue Authority (TRA) the responsibility to collect levies. Under new legislation, the TRA will now collect a new combined "skills and development" levy, based on 6 percent of payroll; two thirds will accrue to the treasury and one third will pass directly to the training fund. Given pressures from the treasury to secure maximum public general revenues from this source, it is expected that the TRA will collect the levy more vigorously, particularly in terms of employer registration and follow-up on payment default.

Clause 19.2 in the new legislation seems to tilt the power and control over the levy strongly toward the Ministry of Finance. Under this clause, the

Minister of Finance (rather than the Minister of Labour) will now "make regulations relating to the collection of the levy." More important, that clause gives new powers to the Minister of Finance to make regulations concerning the *distribution of the levy.* This could carry dangers for the security of the use of the levy for training purposes; until now, VETA, not government, made decisions on the use of levy funds. And an open question remains whether the joint collection of the two levies under a common framework will endanger the security of VETA income over the long term.

Payroll levies: an oversheltered source of funding?

We have noted a number of cases in SSA where the payroll levy system has not resulted in more training, as levy proceeds have been dissipated into general government revenues. This is true in Gabon, Togo and, for a period, in Côte d'Ivoire, leading to a collapse of the training funds that they financed. But more often, payroll taxes have been a stable form of funding for training in SSA countries, and have brought additional funding to the public sector and, in many cases, have been a useful device for offering incentives for the development and strengthening of enterprise training.

Training taxes may constitute an *over*sheltered source of funding, however, causing unspent surpluses (Dougherty and Tan 1991). The Zimbabwe scheme has resulted in income generation far in excess of cost-reimbursement demands, leading to questionable forays into fields loosely related to the objectives of the scheme. Surpluses generated by the scheme in Mauritius have led to a drastic cutting of complementary government funding for the training fund. The initial levy rate may be set too high, especially in the case of cost-reimbursement schemes, or a rate that may have been appropriate at one time is not revised downwards as financing needs change. In Nigeria, the levy rate, initially set at 3 percent in 1971, was reduced subsequently to the current rate of 1 percent four years later. Surpluses may lead to inefficiencies and top-heavy bureaucracies; alternatively, they may lead to the use of payroll tax revenues for purposes other than training. Herein lies the role of strong controlling boards, representing the major stakeholder interests, to monitor the system and to ensure that abuse does not ensue.

The problem, however, arises from the arbitrary way in which levy rates are fixed and from the inflexibilities of the system (with the tax rate often prescribed in the legislation setting up the scheme). In the initial stages of setting up a scheme, frequently the levy rate is fixed arbitrarily. Often, the pragmatic approach adopted is to ask how much the system (that is, employers) will bear and to emulate current rates in other countries rather than to estimate revenue needs (which may change in the future), from which an initial tax rate is derived. This highlights the basic dilemma: How can a payroll tax system be made flexible enough to respond to changing expenditure needs (and avoid surpluses), without forgoing the benefit of stable funding? It would be advisable to include within the enabling legislation a requirement to review the levy rate periodically (say, every four to five years), but to guarantee a stable levy rate between revision dates.

Lessons for policy

Training levies: strengths and limitations

Training taxes, usually levied as a percentage of company payrolls, are now the most pervasive mechanism employed for funding training systems throughout the world (Whalley and Ziderman 1990). Training levies have been introduced in many SSA countries and are on the policy agenda in a number of others. But SSA countries have had less overall success with training levies than other regions—the schemes have worked well in some SSA countries, but not in others. In this policy-oriented chapter, we draw up a balance sheet (based on National Business Initiative 1995), setting out the strengths and advantages of training levies against their possible dangers and limitations (Table 6.3).

Issues in levy scheme design

Table 6.4 summarizes a number of crucial issues in payroll levy scheme design and implementation; failure to pay due attention to these issues is likely to compromise the prospects for successful operation of the payroll levy scheme.

Table 6.3 Payroll Levies: Advantages and Limitations

Advantages	Limitations
Diversifies the revenue base for financing training, by mobilizing additional revenues	Given their particular training needs, many firms, particularly small ones, do not benefit from the scheme; this breeds resentment, opposition, and compromises the status of training levies as "benefit taxation"
Can provide a stable and protected source of funding for national training provision; this is particularly important in the context of national budgetary instability	Earmarked taxation does not conform well with the principles of sound public finance and weakens attempts to unify the national tax system
Where forming part of a levy-grant system, can encourage firms to intensify their training efforts, increase training capacity and raise training quality	Under fiscal pressure, government may incorporate training levy proceeds into general public tax revenues
A strong case can be made for viewing earmarked payroll levies as "benefit taxation"	Levy proceeds may be diverted to non-training uses
Training levies collected from formal sector employers can serve as a vehicle for cross subsidization of training, especially from the formal to the informal sector	Payroll levies may constitute an over-sheltered source of funding, leading to unspent surpluses, inefficiencies, and top-heavy bureaucracies
	Payroll levies raise the cost of labor to the employer, possibly discouraging employment
	Employers may shift the incidence of the levy on to workers in the form of lowered wages; in this case, workers and not the employers bear the burden of the tax

Table 6.4 Issues in Levy Scheme Design and Implementation

Issue	Commentary
Levy rate	Levy rates to be subject by law to periodic review to avoid accumulation of surpluses
National or sectoral levy rates	A standard, national payroll levy rate (rather than differing sectoral rates) will be most appropriate for most SSA country situations
Sectoral coverage	Levy coverage should be as wide as possible across economic sectors and to include public enterprises, NGOs, etc.
Company size	Very small firms should be exempt from levy payment, on both efficiency and equity grounds
Levy collection	Levy collection should be placed in the hands of effective agents; self-collection by funding organization to be avoided
Security of levy proceeds	Special attention should be given to guarding levy revenues from raiding by the government (especially where tax authorities act as the collection agent), by placing in special, closed accounts
Employers buy-in	Employers should be involved in payroll levy policy formation and execution
Avoidance of premature introduction of payroll levies	Payroll levies may be inappropriate where levy-income generating capacity is weak—either because of the limited size of the formal sector or administrative/organizational difficulties of levy collection

CHAPTER 7

Finance Mechanisms: Augmenting Funding for Training

Funding augmentation versus funding distribution

Two central financing issues are common to all training systems. The first concerns the need to augment the total amount of funding for public sector training in view of a paucity of government funding. This is in part the result of structural adjustment policies and increasing demands on government funding from competing sectors. The second relates to improving the effectiveness of national training systems to better meet the needs of society and the economy. Governments have increasingly turned to various financing mechanisms—some well established, others largely experimental—to achieve these objectives.

Policies for augmenting the amount of resources available for training programs may entail a combination of such measures as greater funding diversification, reduced government training subsidization, and increased sharing of the financial burden by other beneficiaries, particularly trainees and enterprises. Funding mechanisms that lead to better training outcomes and other national policy objectives usually relate to the allocation of training resources and transfers within the system. This distinction between financing mechanisms that increase the total amount of funding resources available to the training system as a whole and those mechanisms that allocate given funding resources (Johanson 1995) is useful for gaining a better understanding of the objectives and functioning of various training finance mechanisms. The distinction should not be pressed too far, however, and is best seen as a useful, but not perfect, pedagogic device. Some financing mechanisms relate both to augmenting finance resources and to their transfer within the training system (for example, training levies), while others do not fit into either category.

In this chapter we discuss mechanisms aimed at funding augmentation; the focus is on augmenting funding for institutional training. The following chapter deals with funding distribution.

Funding diversification: alternative approaches

In national training systems where public training budgets are constrained, it is usual practice to seek alternative or additional funding for public training from other sources, a process that is referred to in the literature as funding diversification. The process is outlined in Figure 7.1.

The left side of the figure illustrates the situation where public sector training providers, the dominant suppliers of institutional training, are funded by public budgetary allocations. The introduction of funding diversification may take different forms. The figure identifies four main

Figure 7.1. Alternative Approaches for Funding

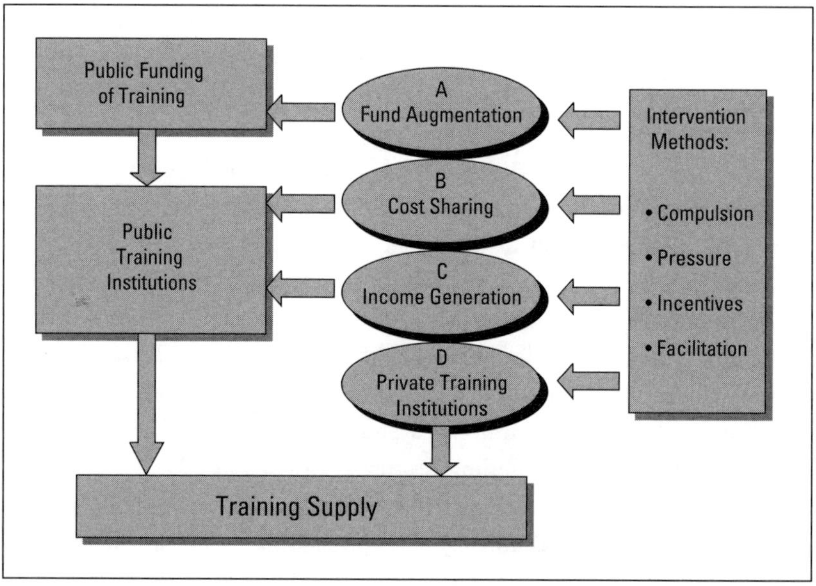

avenues that may be pursued, separately or in parallel; three are direct and one is indirect.

First, as shown by ellipse A, public sector training funds available for the support of training institutions via subventions may be augmented from other sources; the classic method is to impose special taxes, earmarked for training. Here, the size of the pool of funds available for distribution to training institutions is augmented, but there is no immediate effect on the income of individual training institutions. The second approach (ellipse B) is to lighten the weight of training finance falling on public funds through the introduction of cost sharing with the beneficiaries of training. This is achieved mainly by introducing training course fees or by raising them to more realistic levels. These measures will allow a reduction in public subsidies for training or the provision of more or better training services with given levels of public support. User fees could be used also to augment public financing, such as through payment for needed quality improvements or even basic supplies, without reducing public financing. In these cases, there is a direct change in the sources of funding for the core training activities of the institution, with trainee fees partially replacing public funding (but not always, as we shall argue below). Third, (ellipse C), training institutions may seek additional income from other sources, such as by selling products or renting out facilities. In this case, income generation, if sizable, is not related directly to the institution's central core training activities (see below).

A fourth, indirect method of generating funding for training (and, in parallel, reducing the call on public funds) is through the development of private training institutions—ellipse D. This approach may be particularly relevant for country cases where expansion of the training system is desirable. Expansion can be achieved through the growth of private rather than public training provision, without large commitments of public funds. We discuss each of these four methods in turn.

Fund augmentation

Training levies

As noted in Chapter 6, many countries now use special training taxes to generate funding for the public financing of training. Earmarked training taxes, levied on the payrolls of enterprises, have become the most widely adopted alternative to government budgetary allocations. In many cases, the declared intention underlying the introduction of a payroll levy is to lighten public sector financing burdens. However, there remains the danger that, because of funding pressures from other areas of government activity, this process may be taken further than intended.

Levy income drives out government funding—Tanzania. The Tanzanian levy provides a case in point: levy income has displaced government funding of capital and development expenditure. Under the Strategic Action Plan accompanying the establishment of VETA and the Tanzanian training levy, it was envisaged that government would no longer fund recurrent public training expenditures. Operational expenses to run the new system would be borne by revenue generated through the system's own resources—levy income, fees, and other generated income. However, for the foreseeable future, capital and development expenditure would continue to be funded by government and donors; indeed, continuing government funding support is envisaged in the Vocational Education and Training Act (1964). Government found it expedient to opt out of public financing of training altogether, passing the burden of capital development funding onto VETA. Moderate government contributions to capital development were forthcoming for the first two years of operation; in 1997 government allocations to VETA were phased out completely. Concurrently, donor contributions are being scaled down and constitute only about 55 percent of budgeted capital and development expenditure for the year 2000; the shortfall is provided from VETA internally generated revenues rather than from government allocations.

Levy income complements government funding—Mauritius. The Tanzanian case may be contrasted with the more positive experience in Mauritius. Here also, the major part of the levy raised is used directly by the Industrial and Vocational Training Board (IVTB) for its own training programs. But the government matches, from general revenues, employer levy contributions to the IVTB for recurrent expenditure, and pays 85 percent of capital expenditure by the IVTB (Dar, Gill and Bredie 1997); donor funding is minor. Thus, during a period of major IVTB expansion, it was the government that provided the bulk of IVTB overall funding directly through general government revenues. This situation may now be in a process of change, because of the accumulation of nonrefunded levies (traditionally, only about a quarter of levy income was redistributed back to companies, though recently this has risen dramatically). Beginning in the financial year 1997/78, the IVTB was called upon to use part of its considerable reserves; as a result the government contribution has fallen substantially. In 1998, the government contribution was set at a token level only, as a signal to the IVTB that it should reduce substantially its accumulated reserves. With the rundown of accumulated fund surpluses, the way is open for renewed government financing.

Levy income replaces government subsidy of enterprise training. Although this chapter focuses on augmenting funding for training institutions, training levies may lighten the burden of training finance falling on public budgets in a different way. We have noted in Chapter 3 the tendency for enterprises, particularly in the formal sector, to undertrain. In response, the state may provide a framework of training subsidies (for initial training, including apprenticeships, management courses, and continuing training more generally), thereby offering incentives to enterprises to train more and better. Levy-grant mechanisms offer an alternative funding source for these training incentives, with the government-financed training subsidy being replaced by compulsory enterprise-funded training grants/cost reimbursement (see Chapter 9 for a further discussion).

Provision of training services

A training fund may generate limited additional incomes by providing services for payment to enterprises; these include consultancy, the development of training manuals, training promotion, advisory, and other services.

Cost sharing

Unlike fund augmentation, which results in a larger funding pool, cost sharing aims at reducing the size of allocations to individual training institutions. A general approach, which seems to be more prevalent in advanced rather than developing economies, is that of matching funds.

However, the best known and most widely used method by far, is the imposition, or raising the level, of user fees to trainees or students enrolled in training courses.

Matching funds

The use of matching funds (often referred to as cofinancing) requires that the institution in receipt of public funds assume responsibility for raising part of training costs, particularly for capital investments. Thus, not only do institutions receive less than full funding from budgetary sources, but they are also obliged (as a condition for the receipt of public allocations) to finance some proportion of training from their own sources. This approach does not specify how this funding should be raised, and the most straightforward approach is for training institutions to pass on the unsubsidized portion of training costs to the beneficiaries in terms of fees. But institutions may also respond to cofinancing arrangements by generating income from other sources (see below), though this is not strictly cost sharing.

Matching funds not only supplement public funding; but they may also encourage local initiative in generating funding, with local institutions that wish to receive government funding embarking on revenue generation activities (Bolina 1994). The approach offers flexibility, with the option of varying the proportion of required institutional matching by region, institution, or course offering in line with defined policy (Jager and Buhrer 2000); also, the matching proportion may be raised over time, as institutions gain strength in revenue generation.

An indirect, and nonobligatory, variant to cofinancing is available; while it is different in conception, similar results may be achieved. Institutions are provided with less than full budget allocations (based on standard costs elements) and are thus under pressure, though not obliged, to supplement income from other sources. This approach underlies the budgeting of public training institutions in Tanzania, discussed below.

Cost recovery: user fees

It is legitimate to require trainees to bear at least a part of the costs of training when skills acquisition is seen as an investment in human capital, with the promise of higher labor market earnings and a greater probability of sustained employment. Many SSA countries—including Malawi, Madagascar, Mauritius, Nigeria, Tanzania, Zambia, and Zimbabwe—have introduced fees for training courses. Fees are usually set at symbolic levels only; fee income accruing to the IVTB in Mauritius accounts for only 1 to 2 percent of revenue. In some cases, however, fees are more substantial, even though still far from full cost-recovery. In public training centers in Tanzania, fee levels are about 15 percent of recurrent costs; in Madagascar, 27 percent.

The efficacy of cost recovery through user fees will depend to no small extent on overall training fee policy. We may discuss user fee policy within two very different contexts. A central body, whether government or training authority, may impose standard user fees across training institutions. Alternatively, training institutions may be granted the freedom to introduce, and fix the level of, fees for training courses provided. While both produce the desired effect of greater cost recovery and of lowering pressures on public budgets, they carry different implications for the management and functioning of training systems.

Standard, nationally set compulsory fees (as are in place in public training centers in Tanzania, for example) are unlikely to reflect local market realities. They obviate the use, by individual institutions, of user fee policy as a management device, especially in terms of marketing various available courses to client groups with differing needs. Centralized fixing of standard fees is also an inflexible tool; it does not allow the local institution to vary fees to reflect changing local market conditions.

In cases where user fees are voluntary and left to local institutional initiative, they may encourage training providers to develop a more dynamic, even aggressive, approach to exploiting the potential of the local market environment. In this way institutional fee policy becomes more than a device for cost recovery and cost sharing: In providing a mechanism for varying fee levels across courses and client groups it serves as a tool for moving the training system toward an environment characterized by open, demand-oriented training. However, there is an important proviso here: Local training institutions should be free to retain user fee income and the sums collected should not be deducted from institutional budgetary allocations. In many cases, this condition has not been met: in Zambia; fees collected at the technical training institutes, while easing the immediate cash flow, do not add to net institutional income. More generally, it is recognized that fee policy is not set in a vacuum. Institutional-level fee fixing is usually just one element (ideally a central one) of more general, decentralized training systems with local institutional autonomy. It is only in this more liberal context that the full potential of cost sharing is likely to be realized.

Finally, the positive financial benefits from greater cost recovery need to be examined alongside the potentially adverse effects on equity. Higher, realistic fees will exclude from training those who are unable to pay; fees set at comfortably low levels will not make a sizable contribution to cost recovery. In particular, negative impacts on the access to training opportunities of the poor, minorities, rural populations, and other disadvantaged groups are likely to ensue. This points to the widely recognized need to introduce targeted subsidies directed to these at-risk groups, in the form of scholarships and reduced fees. However, targeting those *most* in need within these groups, particularly in the SSA context, has proved difficult. A form of creaming is likely to result as subsidies more readily reach those less obviously in need, on the margin of the eligibility threshold.

Trainee loans

Cost-sharing schemes, using user fees, are likely to be burdensome not only for the poor, thus discouraging participation in formal training programs; this is particularly so if fees are set at a sufficiently high level to achieve significant cost recovery. The classic solution to this problem, encountered most frequently in higher education, is deferred cost recovery (Albrecht and Ziderman 1991). Loans can provide students with the means to pay tuition fees (and living expenses); thus, they ease student payment burdens during study by enabling them to delay payment until they are in receipt of the higher earnings that the education course has made possible. In similar fashion, there is increasing support for the use of training loans schemes as an adjunct to raising fees for training programs; however, more sober reflection militates against this (Herschbach 1993).

There are a number of reasons why training loans (which have been introduced in a number of Western countries, including the United Kingdom) are unlikely to be appropriate for SSA training systems. The track record for student loan schemes, particularly in SSA countries, is poor. Student loan schemes, introduced in Kenya, Tanzania, and Zimbabwe, for example, have all resulted in low loan recovery, largely because of overly generous repayment conditions, including below-market rates of interest, repayment in nominal terms, and long grace periods. In addition, given the presence of administrative costs and repayment default, a regime of student grants may be more cost-effective than loans. The sound administration of a loans scheme requires appropriate, high-level institutional support—at a premium in many SSA countries. Given the lack of success in administering student loan schemes in SSA, it is improbable that training loans would fare better. At present, they do not appear as a realistic option over the medium term.

Income generation by providers

Income from production

In many training programs, income is generated from the sale of production and service activities of trainees. Such income generation may take many forms. Income may be derived from the training process itself. This could be in the form of the provision of services (such as car repair or hairdressing services), which also offers trainees valuable practical experience gained from working with real clients. Or, items produced as part of training may be sold. Income additions are likely to be marginal from these sources.

But it is possible to utilize available skills and facilities to produce output for sale in the local market. While the concept of combining learning with practical experience is maintained, the issue becomes one of balance between these two activities (Herschbach 1993). As more weight is given to instruction, the income potential from production declines. Alternatively, quality of training might suffer as emphasis is placed on production rather than instruction. Against this, however, exposure to local markets may lead to market-oriented training.

The proportion of recurrent expenses that can be covered by production sales may vary considerably from case to case; but while there are some exceptions to the contrary, the scope for cost recovery is limited, usually accounting for only a small percentage of recurrent expenditure. In some cases, however, it can contribute a considerable proportion of total costs; Herschbach (1993) suggests as much as 80 percent for Swaziland. In the case of the Botswana Brigades, training with production has been able to recover, on average, 20 percent of total training cost (Franz, Maleta, and Mtambo 1998). The recovery potential for the Brigades has not been fully exploited; Franz (2000) assesses this to be in the range of 25 to 35 percent of total costs and, in exceptional cases, even higher. But a major objection, often voiced in relation to the Botswana Brigades, is that training institutions may be competing unfairly with the local companies because of their low labor-input costs (Franz 2000).

As with training fee policy, local initiative in income generation from production will be stunted if this income does not contribute to institutional budgets. In Zimbabwe, for example, income from production accrues to the training fund, not the training institution.

Sale of services

Training institutions may generate income from the sale of services, including the renting out of underused facilities and providing consulting services to local enterprises.

Encouraging private provision

This chapter is concerned with the financing burden falling on government in supporting public training institutions. Why is private training provision important in this context? Responding to pressures for the expansion of formal, institutional training provision will require sizable increases in public expenditures. These increases, we have argued, could be contained by additional, offsetting revenues generated from increases in course fees at public training institutions.

A complementary measure is to encourage the growth of private training institutions, with trainees paying full costs. In this way, expansion of the national training system can be achieved, but through the growth of private rather than public training provision—and without commitments of public funds. Indeed, if there are financial constraints holding back private institutions' development, it may be cost-effective for the government to provide public subsidies to these institutions. In this way, government could facilitate national training provision with a minimal burden on the public purse (or, at least, at lower cost than expansion of the public training system). In addition, of course, *reduced* public training provision could be possible (and concomitant budgetary reductions), with the reduction in public training supply made up by expansion of private training institutions.

In many countries, the lack of private training provision results from financial, institutional, and other constraints holding back private provider development. Chapter 3 noted that training provision in public training institutions might be a justifiable response to a lack of private training providers. But in some countries this lack of development in private training supply may be more a response to government training policy than it is its cause. Thus, despite the important role that private training institutions can play in meeting growing demands for skills training, governments often treat these institutions with a large degree of skepticism.

The imposition of restrictions such as legal prohibitions, tight regulatory control, and tuition fee ceilings may combine to impede private institutional start-up. While these restrictions are intended to protect the interests of potential trainees, they are often counterproductive in constraining private training supply. A more liberal regulation regime aimed at quality control is needed, combined with an enabling environment that encourages the incipient private training institutions.

In considering steps that governments might take to encourage private institutional training supply, it is necessary to ask: Why is private provision not forthcoming, and what are the constraints? We discuss these issues in the following paragraphs.

Measures for building up private training capacity

Four types of constraints hold back the development of private training institutions: financial constraints, fee policy issues, regulation and control of private training institutions, and information gaps (Table 7.1).

Financial constraints. The large majority of private training institutions in SSA countries offer courses in commercial and business occupations, with

Table 7.1 Constraints on the Development of Private Training Capacity

Constraint	Mitigation
Financial	To offset limited capital market access, offer development loans/subsidies
	Provide subsidies for equipment and staff development
Fee policy	Avoid imposing protective training tuition fee ceilings, without good cause
Regulation	Be sparing in regulatory and enforcement policies
Consumer information	Provide good information to potential trainees on the quality of institutions and course offerings
	Provide updated information on relevance of courses to labor market demands and opportunities

comparatively low capital costs and an adequate supply of instructors. Costs of technical and industrial courses, however, are higher, particularly for capital development.

Fees policies. Imposed tuition fee ceilings, while aimed at protecting trainees from exploitive activities by private training institutions, may limit the ability of these institutions to enter new training markets, especially those with high investment and recurrent costs. Moreover, tight (low-level) fee control may produce the undesirable effect of low-cost, low-quality training.

Regulatory environment. Private training institutions are unlikely to flourish in an overly strict regulatory environment. Regulation is no doubt required against the possibility of dishonest practices, excessive advertising, and low-quality training. However, regulation and enforcement should be sparing; while sufficiently robust to counter excesses, they should be designed to encourage private training institutions to operate fairly and efficiently within a facilitating, regulatory environment.

Consumer information. Without reliable information, consumers are unable to make wise and informed choices. But relevant information on private training institutions is often lacking. This lacuna may provide an opportunity for government to provide potential trainees with information on both the quality and stability of private training institutions. Provision of updated information on the relevance of courses to labor market demands and job opportunities is also important.

Role of government: four intervention modes

Clearly, significant funding diversification does not take place in a vacuum. There is a role for active government policy in the development of all four methods of funding diversification. Yet, government moves to increase funding diversification may take a number of forms; we find it useful to distinguish among four intervention modes, on a continuum of decreasing government intervention: compulsion, pressure, incentives, and facilitation. The relationship between intervention mode and method of funding diversification is mapped in Table 7.2. There is a clear relationship between the mode of government intervention and the method of funding diversion employed. Those cases where there is a strong effect of a given intervention mode on funding diversification method lie on or near the diagonal in the table.

Training taxes, whether levied on company payrolls, output, or other measure, constitute the mechanism usually employed for fund augmentation. By definition, training taxes are compulsory, though in practice tax evasion may be an option where collection mechanisms are weak. This is the case with payroll levies in Tanzania and Zimbabwe. Thus, compulsion is a strong element in policies aimed at fund augmentation. In some instances attempts at resource augmentation have resulted from government pressure, direct or indirect, rather than compulsion. For example, under the former industrial training board system in South Africa the lack of government measures to support enterprise training led to voluntary attempts at funding augmentation at the sectoral level via levies; these voluntary methods were less than successful.

Table 7.2 Funding Diversification: The Role of Government Policy

	Method of Funding Diversification			
Intervention Mode	Fund augmentation	Cost sharing	Income generation	Private training institutions
Compulsion	Strong	Strong		
Pressure	Weak	Strong	Strong	
Incentives		Weak	Weak	Strong
Facilitation				Strong

Note: a blank indicates "not applicable" or "of marginal importance."

Both compulsion and pressure modes figure strongly in policies aimed at greater cost sharing. In many cases the major form of cost recovery is through centrally imposed institutional training fees. Alternatively, pressures from tight institutional budgets (cutting or containing present levels of support) may lead training providers to seek sources of additional income generation through raising training fees. Incentives, such as institutional retention of generated fee income, may act as a trigger leading to greater cost recovery, but these effects are not strong. Usually, compulsion is not an element of policies aimed at the generation of income by training institutions. But, as with cost sharing, pressures from constrained institutional budgets lead to income generation. Incentives (such as retaining generated income) can play a role in encouraging institutions to augment income, but not a strong one. Finally, private sector training development may respond to government policies. In particular, government subsidies for private training institutions (albeit set at a lower level than support for public training institutions) are likely to offer strong incentives for private sector training development. But of no less importance is the role of government as a facilitator: to ensure that the institutional environment is conducive to private sector growth.

Responding to budgetary pressure: institutional income in Tanzania

As already noted, the Tanzanian training authority, VETA, has neglected the development of private training capacity; however, it has achieved more success in cost sharing and income generation.

VETA owns and funds the network of public training centers, mainly through a 2 percent payroll levy. This network consists of 10 Regional Vocational Training and Service Centers (RVTSCs) that service the overall training needs of the regions, 7 smaller vocational training centers (VTCs), and the Morogoro Vocational Teachers Training College (MVTTC). The annual budget for each VETA-owned institution includes two income heads, for "school fees" and for "other income generation," respectively. The *school fees* category comprises mainly fees for attending training courses, but also other items such as trade testing and application fees. Other income includes rental income (from renting out facilities) and generated income from student projects and training with production.

Each institution is expected to generate the sums designated under these two budget heads. If these sums are not forthcoming, the institution is not given compensating allocations by VETA, and institutions will need to accommodate the shortfall with reduced expenditures. Budgeted self-sufficiency rates vary across institutions; in 2000 it was set at 40 percent (of budgeted recurrent expenditure) for MVTTC, and ranged from 11 to 39 percent for RVTSCs and from 7 to 22 percent for VTCs. Overall, income from these two sources constituted 27 percent of budgeted institutional income in 2000; 15 percent from school fees and 12 percent from other income generation. This level is up from about a fifth in 1999; indeed, it is understood that it is VETA policy to raise the self-sufficiency rate to 40 percent over the medium term.

The system exerts indirect pressure on institutions to ensure that budgeted incomes from outside sources are, indeed, collected. Scope for institutional initiative, however, varies by type of income source. While most school fees are set centrally by VETA and are standard, as is often the case in other countries, there is still scope for raising total fee income by increasing trainee enrollments. Thus, in 1999 some centers raised school fee income though an increase in enrollment resulting from the introduction of double shifts. Fees for short courses are negotiable locally, as are the various other income categories. Overall, it would seem that the system is working; the budget statement for 2000 reports that, overall, income received from these two categories was in close conformity with budgeted income. Outcome variation, however, is likely across institutions.

Discussions are currently under way on plans for the decentralization of the VETA framework, envisaging moves toward considerable local autonomy, especially for the RVTSCs; hopefully, this will also include greater institutional autonomy in the setting of user fees.

Lessons for policy

This chapter presented four options for the diversification of funding to public sector institutional training, with a view to reducing the financing burden falling on public budgets. We noted that these options operate in different ways (Figure 7.1): three act directly in bringing in additional revenues to the training sector, while the fourth affects training budgets only indirectly. Thus, additions to total funding available for allocation to training providers may be secured through the levying of payroll taxes. Again, training institutions may augment public budgetary allocations through cost sharing (in particular through introducing or raising course fees) and through income generation (largely from combining production with training). And, finally, encouragement may be given to the development of private training institutions.

These diversification options are not alternatives; all four avenues may be explored simultaneously. However, whether to do so remains a policy issue; this will depend on a number of factors, including the feasible scope of the intervention and the balance between the advantages and weaknesses of the approach, in each case. We now turn to a consideration of these issues in relation to a major variant of each of the four options.

Scope for funding diversification

The dominant tool for augmenting funds is the training levy. The scope for levying payroll taxes is well established by international experience in SSA countries and elsewhere. Almost all countries that have introduced payroll levies have set the levy rate in the range of 1 to 2 percent of company payroll bills, the majority at the lower end of the range.

There is considerably less conformity of practice in raising tuition fees to increase cost sharing or of training institutions generating income from production. This should come as no surprise. The feasibility for tuition fee setting (in relation to unit costs of training) is a compound of many factors, which vary from place to place. They include (a) type and costs of training, (b) the price elasticity of trainee demand for different training courses, (c) political constraints, (d) policies for equality of opportunity, and (e) student aid to assist disadvantaged students unable to meet the new, augmented fee levels.

In similar fashion, the scope for generating income from production by training institutions will also depend on local factors, including the nature of the product, local demand conditions, and potential market competition. Thus, it is not possible to be prescriptive in relation to the scope for generating revenues from tuition fees or for augmenting income through production combined with training. These issues will need to be settled on a case-by-case basis.

Diversification mechanisms: strengths and weaknesses

Table 7.3 lists the major advantages and risks of the four options for funding diversification.

Table 7.3 Mechanisms for Funding Diversification: Advantages and Risks

Mechanism for funding diversification	Leading policy variant	Income accrues to:	Advantages	Risks
Fund Augmentation:	Training levies	Public sector/ training funds	Diversifies the revenue base for financing training, by mobilizing additional revenues Can provide a stable and protected source of funding for national training provision	See listing in Table 6.3
Cost Sharing:	Raising tuition fees	Training institutions	Will make training more cost-effective as training institutions vie to attract trainees. Training will become more demand oriented	Imposes hardship on disadvantaged students, depending on scope of scholarship policy. Income may not remain with the training institution.
Income Generation:	Income from production	Training institutions	May lead to training outcomes more closely geared to the needs of the market	Neglect of the training function, lowering the quality and quantity of training. Too many resources may go to production rather than training. Income may not remain with the training institution.

Private Training Provision	—	No income generation—budgetary savings to public sector/ training funds	Expansion of the national training system can be achieved—and without commitments of public funds.	The concentration of private providers on low cost, high demand courses, may leave public sector institutions with the more costly, technical courses and limited possibilities for across-course subsidization

CHAPTER 8

Funding Distribution: Transfers to Training Institutions

This chapter deals with the criteria used for institutional funding. For simplicity, we present the discussion in terms of the institutional allocation of funding by government. However, the argument is equally applicable to situations where a training fund (financed by government, training levies, or both) replaces the government as the body responsible for financing training institutions.

The allocation among training providers of the total government training budget is a major component of the financing system in all three training market scenarios discussed above, not the least in conventional training markets (as shown in Figure 4.1). In many countries, a clearly formulated, transparent disbursement policy is lacking. Yet, the mechanism through which government transfers funds to training institutions is likely to have an important effect on the way in which this funding is used and on institutional behavior more generally. In particular, we shall argue that inherent shortcomings in the transfer mechanisms may promote low internal efficiency of training institutions and a strengthening of supply-driven training provision.

Direct allocation mechanisms

The methods currently used for the *direct* allocation of state funding to public training institutions vary widely across SSA countries; we subsequently consider indirect, student-based funding. These direct funding transfer methods may be grouped under three broad categories (see Ziderman and Albrecht 1995 for a fuller discussion of institutional funding at the university level). Funding allocation may be based on objective criteria relating to the internal workings of the training institutions—either to the outputs of the training institution or to its inputs. More generally, however, governments eschew the use of internally related objective criteria (inputs or outputs); we group these other methods together as ad hoc funding.

Ad hoc funding

We include under ad hoc funding such widespread practices as incremental funding, where institutional allocations are based on those of the previous year, often augmented by across-the-board incremental budgetary increases or perhaps, according to political influence, interest group pressure or the negotiating skills of the institutional actors. Such ad hoc systems of allocation, rooted as they are in the status quo, are unlikely to facilitate internal efficiency or market-oriented dynamism. Indeed, a major defect of ad hoc funding is that it provides no incentive for institutional efficiency. Clearly, if funding is unrelated to the internal activities of the training provider, there are no incentives built into the funding system to promote greater efficiency—and generally results in the opposite. The other major shortcoming of ad hoc funding—one that is shared, we shall argue, with input- and output-based funding—is that it does nothing to encourage training providers to be adaptive to labor market needs; training provision remains static and supply driven.

Ad hoc funding in Zambia. The 23 trades training institutes in Zambia are funded by the Ministry of Science, Technology, and Vocational Training (MSTVT), through largely ad hoc funding methods. Institutes present annual budget requests to the MSTVT. Initial institutional allocations are based on the previous year's budgetary allocation (with an allowance for inflation), but subsequently adjusted downwards to reflect the lower total budgetary allocation approved by the Ministry of Finance. The upshot is that salary allocations for permanent staff continue to absorb almost the entire budget for recurrent expenditures, leaving little available for materials, supplies, and maintenance. A recent independent (restricted circulation) review of training finance in Zambia concluded that this funding approach has encouraged complacency among training providers because funding is secured regardless of performance, and little attention is accorded to training quality or provision relevance.

Input-based funding

A more objective alternative is to fund institutions on the basis of the estimated costs of inputs required for training provision. The simplest, but least satisfactory, form of input funding is to base allocations on itemized budgets for future years that are submitted by training institutions. Since overall budget allocation for each institution is based on approval of individual expenditure items, this form of funding leads to inflexible line-item budgeting, restricting the use of funding only for approved purposes.

A more flexible form of input funding derives institutional allocations from formulas, typically based on trainee enrollments or number of classes. The most common approach is to multiply enrollments by a parameter of unit costs; formulas may be enriched to take account of the differing cost of various training courses. Governments may use input formulas as a form of indirect control over enrollment patterns by employing differential weightings (or coefficients) based on course offering or student background. In the latter case, the funding formula can facilitate the achievement of policy goals by encouraging training institutions to seek out and admit disadvantaged youngsters, the unemployed, and minority groups. In linking funding to the cost of training activities, input funding secures a far greater level of accountability than is forthcoming under ad hoc allocation.

Two inherent problems, however, are associated with input funding. First, there is little incentive for efficiency. Indeed, funding formulas based on average costs provide incentives for institutional expansion, perhaps regardless of trainee suitability; furthermore, they do not offer quality assurance, either in terms of the quality of the training offered or its job relevance. Second, because input budgeting promotes a training environment that is divorced from employment needs and the job market, it may lead to a training system that is out of kilter with the realities of the labor market.

Output-based funding

The concepts of "payment by results" and rewarding performance underlie output-based methods of funding. Output-related funding provides financial incentives to training institutions by rewarding them for meeting certain predetermined levels of training delivery (Felstead 1998); training institutions not achieving these predefined outputs are penalized. Outputs may be measured in absolute terms (often defined as the number of course completions) but may also relate to the speed with which outputs are produced (to minimize cost-enhancing repetition).

The most important benefit to be gained from adopting output-based funding is enhanced efficiency of the training process. Since a training institution's budget is linked to the achievement of particular outputs, an incentive is present for training institutions to change and improve various aspects of their training policies and practice in order to increase their training performance and, hence, funding.

Output versus outcome. Output formula funding as discussed thus far may be appropriate for addressing problems of internal efficiency of training institutions. But it is unlikely to provide a good proxy measure of the labor market prospects of trainees, and does not lead to a better matching of training activities with the needs of the market. In sum, it does not result in a greater demand-driven orientation of training. In this regard, a distinction between two types of performance-related budgeting should be drawn; this distinction is not usually emphasized in the literature. The type of output-based funding considered thus far relates to process, to the internal training activities of the training provider. This may be contrasted with training outcomes, on how well the training programs impact with the labor market. Outcomes may be defined in terms of the success of the training provider in meeting labor market needs; this can be measured by the percentage of course completers placed in jobs and by the speed with which they are absorbed into employment.

Creaming and dredging. Output/outcome measures may lead to "creaming," a process whereby training providers screen out less promising candidates to maximize measured output performance. Creaming is likely to result in the exclusion of the poor, unemployed youth, ethnic minorities, and other disadvantaged groups—the very population segments at which the training program may be aimed. This tendency may be countered in a number of ways. A greater weight could be given in the reward structure to outputs drawn from these disadvantaged populations. For programs aimed at special groups, the government could set upper limits on course eligibility, a practice known as "dredging" (Felstead 1998).

Initial placement versus sustained employment. Inevitably, outcomes will be measured in terms of their success at initial placement of trainees; this may not correspond to the achievement of sustained employment over the long term, the ultimate goal of training programs. Indeed, providers may be encouraged to narrow training content and concentrate on meeting short-term market needs rather than designing more flexible training that is better suited to changing labor market needs (Felstead 1998). It is possible to measure these longer term outcomes through well-designed follow-up studies; indeed, outcome studies of this type should constitute an integral part of evaluation and feedback in all training programs, though many SSA countries may not have the capacity to conduct these studies. However, it may be less than practicable to base payment on measured long-term employment effects, given the additional uncertainties and payment delays this would introduce.

Composite formula funding

In general, the implementation of formula funding methods will require a framework that strikes a balance between the individual institutional response to efficiency incentives (that is, to adjustments to its funding) and the need for annual funding stability. For example, output-oriented funding schemes, while leading to better performance, may result in funding instability, as institutional income will depend on outcomes, which in turn are subject to the vagaries of economic activity. If institutional funding is based solely on performance, year-to-year variations in funding may lead to cash-flow problems, thus complicating (even disrupting) the ongoing training process. And funding uncertainty will discourage institutional initiative and change. Thus, output-based funding is unlikely to be successful if used as the sole criterion for funding.

Formula funding will probably be most effective where broadened to include a number of constituent elements. This composite formula funding could include such elements as institutional inputs, outputs, desired labor market outcomes, and the enrollment of special groups. Individual weightings would be assigned to each element. Weightings would reflect the tradeoff adopted between the need for efficiency incentives and stability; they would conform to the relative importance of each element in terms of the overall objectives of the training program in question. The input element (probably total enrollments) would offer greater institutional funding stability, while the output element would provide incentives for internal efficiency of training institutions. The element reflecting labor market outcomes (say, job placement) would offer rewards for external efficiency of the training and bring the training system closer to market needs. Elements relating to the enrollment of such special groups as the unemployed, poor, and disadvantaged youth would facilitate the achievement of social goals; the inclusion of a higher weighting factor for enrollment of lower-ability trainees would help to offset tendencies toward creaming.

Competitive tendering: unifying training markets

Finally, we need to draw a distinction between the funding of publicly supported training institutions (as discussed thus far) and the method adopted for financing training for more specific target groups, such as those with special needs or from the informal sector. In the latter case, it is common for the government (or a training fund) to provide special funding to public institutions to offer the required training courses, perhaps employing allocation methods of the type discussed above. Increasingly, this funding is made available on the basis of training contracts, between the funding body and the training institution, specifying the range of training services to be provided and, perhaps, measures of success against which final payments are made. However, this approach may lead to irregularities in the allocation of contracts; it provides few pressures on the training system to operate efficiently, at low costs (bringing savings on national training budgets), and usually operates as a "closed shop," largely denying entry to private providers. A system of competitive bidding can offer a framework for avoiding these shortcomings and for providing for a more cost-conscious, competitive environment in training provision, in which private providers can compete on equal terms with public training institutions.

Training contracts for informal sector training—Côte d'Ivoire. The following discussion is adopted from Johanson (2001). In recent years the payroll levy financed Vocational Development Training Fund in Côte d'Ivoire (FDFP) has extended its areas of training support to include training for small firms and the informal sector. The FDFP finances its training programs for target groups under this program through the award of training contracts made to prequalified training providers (from the public and private sector) on the basis of competitive bids. The process of prequalification includes field visits of FDFP staff to training provider applicants and assessment of training capabilities according to particular fields of competence; prequalified training providers constitute the pool from which competitive bids are drawn. A proposed training program is sent to three to six prequalified training providers in the relevant field of competence; a contract is awarded on the basis of the best bid received.

In the past, the FDFP had not employed a process of competition among training providers in the award of contracts, and collusion and irregularities had been rife. The present system of competitive tendering has led to lower unit training costs, compared both with earlier years and with other regular programs supported by the fund. One notable outcome has been the success of private training providers in gaining training contracts. The fear that publicly subsidized training institutions would benefit from an unfair price advantage over private providers has been unfounded; public providers receive only about a quarter of training contracts. There is evidence that the competitive process has been successful in infusing a more entrepreneurial approach among management in public, as well as private, training institutions.

Funding public training delivery—South Africa. Under new financing arrangements currently being put in place in South Africa, budgetary allocations would continue to fund training programs for special groups, including the unemployed and youth, as well as preemployment public sector training. Proposals for the disbursement of public funding for training programs aimed at target groups envisage the removal of protection from public training providers and the introduction of performance-related funding criteria. A new system of competitive tendering for long-term training contracts will be adopted. These measures would put an end to the privileged position of such public sector providers as the regional training centers, in relation to existing and emerging private sector institutions. The system aims at encouraging competition between institutional training providers, both public and private, and would enhance providers' responsiveness to the performance criteria against which public funds are to be allocated.

Indirect allocation: trainee-based funding

While it is current practice in SSA countries for the state to support public training by direct transfer of funds to training institutions (usually through ad hoc methods), in principle an alternative, indirect route is available through subsidies to students/trainees. In earlier chapters we have emphasized the advantages of a labor-market-oriented, demand-driven public training system; one approach toward moving the training system in this direction is through a student-responsive institutional training system with greater cost recovery through higher, more realistic training fees (in concert perhaps with trainee loans). But this may not be socially acceptable or politically practicable; indeed, when labor markets are distorted, resulting in narrow skill differentials and low returns to private investments in training, it may not be feasible (see Middleton, Ziderman and Adams 1993). Moreover, student loans have not proved to be a suitable vehicle in SSA countries for facilitating substantial cost recovery. Thus, government subsidy remains on the agenda.

Vouchers

In principle, it is possible to achieve many of the benefits of a trainee-responsive system without moving strongly away from state subsidies and toward greater cost recovery. Institutional training subsidies could be maintained at present (or other suitable) levels, but channeled through the trainees in terms of training vouchers (or perhaps subsidized loans). Thus, subsidization could take one of two paths (given the level of public subsidy of institutional training deemed appropriate); subsidies could be paid directly to the institutions themselves, as is current practice, or via the trainees. The alternative funding routes are shown in Figure 8.1 (in practice, both paths are likely to be used as complementary approaches). The right-hand side of the figure illustrates direct institutional allocations from government (or a training fund); training is free or offered at nominal fees. Alternatively, the subsidy could be made via the trainees themselves, as shown in the left-hand side of the figure; students would meet tuition fees charged by training institutions, wholly (or in part) through vouchers of entitlement to training courses; we refer to this as trainee-based funding.

Many advantages are claimed for a system of subsidy through student-based vouchers. A central motivation for trainee-based funding is to promote competition among training providers as they compete for trainee enrollments, in terms of type and quality of program and in tuition fee level. Vouchers could be used at private training institutions too, thus increasing market competition and widening trainee choice. The system would lead to greater institutional efficiency and quality, and training that is closer to market needs.

In some respects, student-based funding will appear similar to an input funding formula based on the number of students enrolled. From a purely accounting point of view there may be little difference between whether funds are transferred directly to institutions (on the basis of enrollments) or via a voucher mechanism. However, a vital distinction should be made between the two, in terms of the context within which trainees and institutions make their decisions. A trainee-based funding system operates within an environment that offers real choices to trainees in type, quality, and price of training and, in parallel, where competition between public and private training providers is the norm. Direct funding functions within an environment that is more constricted, in which institutions have less scope to differentiate their offerings and to use resources as they see fit, and students have far more limited choices. As these restrictions are loosened, the system moves from direct to, essentially, indirect funding. What we have called trainee-based funding,

Figure 8.1. Alternative Pathways for Funding Institutional Training

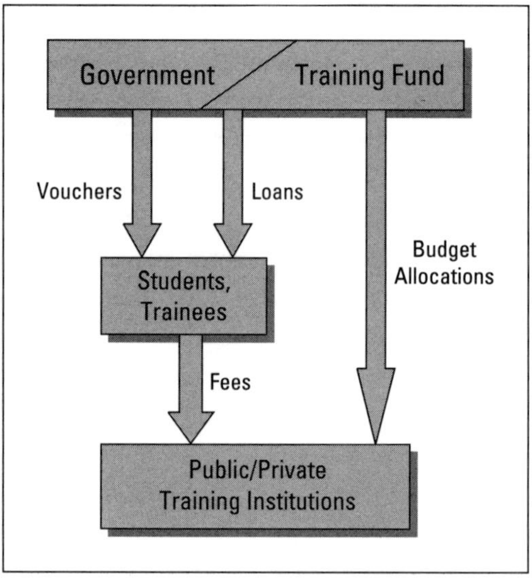

in effect, represents a suitably reformed input-based funding system, in which competition and student choice become the fulcrum of the funding system.

Movement to general student-based funding remains a long way in the future. However, it has an immediate role to play in specific training contexts. Indeed, several countries are using vouchers, in largely experimental programs, as a mechanism for funding training for the informal sector, with the long-term aim of building up demand-driven training markets for informal sector training. The best known example is the voucher program in Kenya providing support for micro and small enterprises. But there are others, including the Mauritius scheme and the flawed intake voucher scheme in Ghana. We shall consider these further in Chapter 10, when we deal with the informal sector.

Policy reform

Ad hoc institutional funding remains the norm in the region; however, it is widely recognized that such, largely arbitrary, funding allocation methods may encourage internal inefficiencies and strengthen tendencies toward supply-driven training. Yet, unlike the case of other desirable training finance reforms, moves toward more objective criteria seem well within the grasp of the governments in many countries, and there has been some promising experimentation with these methods in current training institution reform in the region. Barriers to progress may stem more from institutional resistance, opposition of vested interests, and the slowness of higher education institutions—which would be expected to lead the way in this direction. But, change could well be coming in countries formulating a broader package of institutional reform; objective funding criteria might then constitute part of a more general reform of institutional funding, which would include reduced public funding overall (replaced by cost recovery and income generation), decentralization and enhanced institutional autonomy, and a greater use of contact funding.

CHAPTER 9

Enhancing Enterprise Training

Discussion in Chapter 3 pointed to the tendency for firms to undertrain and some of the underlying reasons therefor. A legitimate response was the offer of training incentives for firms in the form of the direct subsidy of enterprise training by the government. Direct training subsidies could also be provided as part of a levy-grant system. Or, indirect subsidies could be offered through concessions on company tax obligations for firms that train. This chapter discusses these different forms of incentives for company training and considers how successful they may be in improving training outcomes of enterprises.

Direct training subsidies

Government grants versus levy-grant schemes

Some countries offer direct subsidies (out of public funds) to encourage company training. In what ways does this differ from cost reimbursement, as part of a levy-grant scheme? In Chapter 7 we noted that, from the funding side, training levies are beneficial in easing the financing burden on government. On the side of training incentives, also, levy-grant arrangements are likely to be far more efficacious than government-funded training subsidies. With a subsidy scheme, here as in other areas of subsidy, incentives may be indirect and insufficiently focused, failing to catch the attention of senior management. Perhaps too much reliance is placed on the initiative of the individual firms involved—in knowing that the subsidy scheme exists and that the firm is eligible for subsidy, and in overcoming company lethargy and committing to the burdensome process of involvement. But in the case of levy-grant schemes, "involvement" is ensured automatically by the compulsory payment of the levy; anecdotal evidence suggests that senior company finance officers may tend to exert pressure on the training function to ensure that "we get back the levy," through appropriate training provision.

From the viewpoint of the levy-grant scheme (as with government training subsidies), the grant encourages training; but from the firm's standpoint in levy-grant schemes, training recoups the levy! Thus, while there may be a dichotomy between the motivations of the scheme as a whole and that of individual firms, the same end result is achieved: more enterprise training. Moreover, there are likely to be positive long-term effects. The experience of the former U.K. industrial training levy-grant system was that, in time, the process did exert the beneficial effect of increasing training consciousness in the firm; the training function, as a generator of income, becomes more central in the firm's operations.

Finally, we shall argue that one advantage of a well-developed levy-grant scheme over direct government subsidies is that the former is better positioned to adopt a structured, comprehensive approach to training, rather than an ad hoc one. The central lacuna in training underprovision is not only that the amount of training provided is too low, but also that it is often piecemeal and not well integrated.

Efficacy of direct training subsidies

A question often posed when appraising the efficacy of training incentives through grants (from government subsidies or a levy-grant scheme) is whether they result in more training. But, in practice, this question may be an empty one. There are several reasons for this.

First, statistical evidence of additional training may not indicate that the scheme is successful. Unlike the case of revenue-generating levies, where it is readily observed whether public training institutions are training more, the identification of additional enterprise training that genuinely results from training grants is fraught with difficulties. Dougherty and Tan (1991 and 1997) refer to the "repackaging effect," where existing training provision that does not fall within the remit of the incentive scheme is adapted and repackaged to appear to comply with the eligibility requirements for grants. And where there is an increase in the types of training that the scheme sets out to encourage, it may be unclear whether this is a result of the scheme itself or whether it would have been forthcoming anyway. Firms that have consistently adopted positive policies toward training provision in the past will receive windfall benefits; this may be a misallocation of funds unless cost redistribution is an objective of the incentive scheme.

Second, incentive schemes may lead to distortions of the type of training provided. The more extensive the incentives offered by the scheme, the greater would be the enterprise response in additional training. But, by the same token, generous training incentives may now make many types of eligible training profitable to the firm, even though the firm's needs for these training skills may be doubtful. We return to this theme below.

For these reasons we need to be cautious about claims of success made for individual incentive schemes on the basis of increased numbers of workers trained. Little research seems to be available on this issue. Dougherty and Tan (1991) define the lacuna in this way: They argue that we lack studies that "document comprehensively and in detail the training provided by a sample of firms before the introduction of the scheme and afterwards—in other words, what is needed is an in-depth micro approach, rather than the aggregate approach adopted in the literature to date."

Levy-grant schemes

The discussion on payroll levies in Chapter 6 concentrated on the levying side of these schemes; we now focus on aspects of outcomes of the "grant" in levy-grant schemes.

Training off or on the job?

Enterprise training can take on many forms (Chapter 2). Training may be provided in the form of apprenticeship (often divided between training on the job and the attendance at courses provided at an outside training institution).

It may be given wholly on the job as initial or continuing formal training, or training may be less formal and ad hoc, though not necessarily less important to the skills development of the firm. It may be provided off the job, in the form of formal courses for workers, management, or professionals at specialized training institutions. What forms of training should a levy-grant scheme support?

There is a dilemma here. It may be important to encourage certain forms of on-the-job training, but these may be expensive to monitor for quality, and abuse may be difficult to detect. Other forms of training, such as those for professional qualification at recognized external institutions may more readily be subject to surveillance but are not always of highest priority for the firm. This may explain the focus of a number of levy-grant schemes. Apart from apprenticeship training, which is in decline, most training that is recognized for cost reimbursement in the Zimbabwe scheme is training for upgrading or professional qualifications at external institutions; more hands-on, practical training does not receive sizable support. Similar considerations seem to apply to the Kenyan scheme.

Systems approach versus piecemeal reimbursement

A related issue is the breadth of the overall program of training supported by a levy-grant scheme within a firm and its sustainability over the long term. We may recognize two contrasting approaches here. The first, which we may call the "external approach," is typified in the Zimbabwe scheme. Here, a detailed list is produced of approved forms of training and courses that are eligible for rebates; firms are then invited to apply for cost reimbursement for those forms of (mainly external) training that they have sponsored and that match items on the approved list. The latest ZIMDEF list dates back to 1993 and is generally regarded as outdated; it is being revised. But this approach, while offering rebates to firms for certain forms of training and probably encouraging firms to train more (in designated eligible areas) is unlikely to have more than a short-term impact on skills development in the firm and may indeed distort the balance of forms of training provision within the enterprise. This is because it gives recognition and financial support to more standard forms of training—usually provided externally to the firm—that are more readily recognized and monitored (and thus countering potential financial abuse).

An alternative "systems approach"—elements of which are found in the Côte d'Ivoire, Nigerian, and the newly developing South African schemes—takes a broader view. In Côte d'Ivoire, levy exemption and cost reimbursement are contingent on the preparation, and approval by the fund, of a company training plan. In the Nigerian case, grant payment is conditioned on the firm adopting a systematic approach to training based on given criteria; thus, firms are encouraged to think systematically about preparing a training program, defined in terms of their real skill needs, rather than applying for rebates on an ad hoc, short-term basis. This more progressive approach is being developed within the framework of new funding arrangements being put in place in South Africa; to these we now turn.

Disbursement arrangements in South Africa. In South Africa, 80 percent of the proceeds of the new skills development levy is passed on to each SETA in accordance with levy sums paid by employers in each sector; the remainder goes to the National Skills Fund. Uses of moneys received by the SETAs are narrowly prescribed in the annual funding regulations issued by the Department of Labour. The regulations for the first year of operation of the scheme (financial year 2000/01) place a cap on SETA administration and operation cost and exceptional setup costs of 30 percent of levy proceeds (that is, 24 percent of SETA receipts). More relevant to our present discussion, each SETA must distribute back to employers at least 50 percent of levy proceeds as grants.

These grants are of two types: rebates to the employer, based on the levy paid, and discretionary cash grants. Rebates take the following form: employers may receive back 15 percent of the levy for the appointment of a skills development facilitator, 10 percent for the preparation of a workplace skills plan, and a further 20 percent for its implementation. Thus, the emphasis in this first year of operation of the scheme is on planning and developing structured training, in line with identified company needs. Companies are required to carry out a comprehensive training skills needs assessment by identifying their strategic development priorities and mapping in the education and training required to achieve them. Thus, eligible training for rebate is not decided by a central, outside body—as in the external approach mentioned above—but evolves internally in each case through an identification of the skills development needs of individual firms.

SETAs are required to use at least 5 percent of levy income for grants to employers for special skill initiatives in the sector; these grants do not depend on an employer's levy contribution, and individual employers may receive a discretionary grant in excess of 5 percent of levy payment.

Regulations for 2001/02 put more emphasis on levy distribution to employers. Of the 80 percent of levy proceeds received by SETAs, a maximum of 10 percent may now be spent on SETA administration costs while a minimum of 70 percent is recoverable by employers as grants. Prescribed training-related activities eligible for grants include registration of a skills development facilitator and submission of a workplace skills plan (15 percent), implementation of the workplace skills plan (up to 50 percent), and grants for special skills initiatives in the sector (again, at least 5 percent of the total levy).

Indirect subsidies: company tax concessions

In most countries, training expenses incurred by companies are tax deductible, as are expenditures on capital assets. The tax treatment of training expenditures (a form of human capital investment) is typically more favorable than that of machinery and equipment (Dougherty and Tan 1991). Training expenses are tax deductible immediately; whereas physical assets are tax deductible only in installments, over a number of years, through depreciation allowances. However, a training incentive may be given in the form of further tax concessions for company training expenditures in addition to the usual deduction of training expenses for tax purposes. We refer to these as "company tax concessions."

SSA experience with tax concessions

Following Gasskov (1994), most of the literature on the use of company tax credits as an incentive device for enterprise training is concerned with two well-known Latin American examples: the generally successful and extant scheme in Chile and the failed (and phased out) Brazilian scheme. However, there are a number of lesser-known SSA examples of interest, but all generally unsuccessful.

South Africa. The now defunct industrial training board system in South Africa was preceded by a company tax-concession scheme, established under legislation in the 1970s. The scheme allowed for the deduction of 200 percent of training expenditures (reduced to 150 percent in 1984), thus effectively reducing training costs of profitable firms by half (at a corporation tax rate of 50 percent). The scheme was faulted by "gross abuse" of the concession by employers and difficulties in policing claims. Moreover, employer uptake was very low; less than 1 percent of firms in the country claimed these tax concessions for in-service training (National Training Board 1986). It was replaced for a limited period by a system of cash grants, provided to the first industrial training boards by the Department of Labour.

Botswana. In the Botswana scheme, employers are also able to deduct 200 percent of training expenditures from the corporate income tax, effectively reimbursing 70 percent of training costs (Franz 2000). The scheme is virtually unused; employers are largely unaware of the scheme, and procedures are highly complex. Franz (2000) attributes the ineffectiveness of the scheme largely to the fact that the institution granting tax concessions (the Finance Ministry) is not technically competent enough to make decisions on concession eligibility, a problem shared with the South African scheme. Decisions on eligibility for tax deductions were made by the trade testing institution (Madirelo Training and Testing Centre [MTTC]) under the Labour Ministry. "In theory, an employer would need to approach MTTC for approval of its training, and afterwards submit this approval together with the complicated cost statements to the Ministry of Finance ... It is hardly surprising that only a handful of companies had followed this cumbersome procedure" (Franz 2000).

Mauritius. The Mauritius scheme is unusual in Africa in that it operates in tandem with a levy-grant scheme. The presence of two schemes together is not unique; Brazil, for example, also operated both schemes in parallel, though unsuccessfully. What is unusual is the close integration of the two schemes in Mauritius. The combination of tax incentives and levy-grants, under which firms in principle may receive reimbursement of up to 75 percent of training expenditures, has resulted in a complicated training cost reimbursement formula. Firms can receive various levels of tax relief according to the rate of corporate tax that applies to them; the grant from the training fund could bring total relief up to 75 percent of training costs. Thus, firms not liable for corporate tax may receive a reimbursement grant of up to 75 percent of training cost; a firm with a 15 percent tax rate can receive up to 60 percent rebate and deduct an additional 15 percent of training costs from tax obligations. Overall, the administrative and supervisory costs of the scheme are unnecessarily high, which has led to conflict over the interpretation of the rules governing the interrelationship of the two schemes, and, consequently, the reimbursement element of the levy-grant scheme has remained small.

Problems with tax-concession schemes

The major problems with tax-concession schemes are clear. A prerequisite for the introduction of the scheme is a well-developed and broadly based system of corporate taxation, not usually present in SSA countries. Firms with low profits and perhaps poor training capacity do not benefit and are not encouraged to train. Tax-concession schemes only offer benefits to stronger, profitable firms. And, unlike levy-grant schemes, it is the government that bears the cost of these schemes in the form of lost tax revenues; in this sense they are akin to direct training subsidies by the government and may be regarded as representing subsidies in disguise.

Other measures to promote enterprise training

Apprenticeship training

Subsidizing apprentice wages. In many countries, apprenticeship training is a key method of skills development for the formal employment sector. Support for apprenticeship training, in the form of subsidizing the wages of apprentices, often constitutes part of a wider regime of government training subsidies or levy-grant schemes, as described above. A particular case can be made for subsidized apprenticeship wages on both equity and efficiency grounds.

The subsidy of apprentice wages may raise the level of remuneration accruing to trainees. Picking up on themes developed in Chapter 3, the equity case relates to giving parity of treatment to apprentices with their peers (including those in vocational schools) who continue on within the (highly subsidized) formal education system. From the viewpoint of the firm, wage subsidies lower the cost burden of training, in conditions where the costs of apprenticeship training are not passed on fully to the trainee. In calculations of apprenticeship costs in Zimbabwe, Suhr (2000) shows that apprentice wages account for about half of annual gross costs of apprenticeships in the automotive industry. Dougherty and Tan (1991) offer the following efficiency argument for apprenticeship wage subsidies. Subsidized preemployment training at public institutions competes with apprenticeship training. Yet, institutional training may be the less cost-effective training mode; evidence for Zimbabwe is given in Bennell (1993) (see also Ziderman 1989). Increasing the proportion of youngsters taking the apprenticeship route could lead to a net savings in public funds and more cost-effective skills development.

Apprenticeship wage subsidies may be provided in many different ways. They may be offered for the whole of the apprenticeship period as in the Malawi case (see below). Alternatively, wage subsidies may be confined to the earlier years of apprenticeship only, where the net value of apprenticeship output may be low or negative. Thus, in Zimbabwe ZIMDEF finances apprentice wages for the first two years of the four-year training cycle. Support may be particularly appropriate during periods of instruction, off the job, at formal training institutions (where no apprenticeship output is forthcoming).

Apprentice wage subsidies can be a useful tool, positively influencing the quantity of initial training provided by companies; however, a number of preconditions must be present and various pitfalls must be avoided. First, employers may exploit the availability of apprentice wage subsidies to gain access to cheap labor. Second, the elasticity of supply of apprenticeship slots should not be low; if it is, the desired supply response of an increased apprenticeship intake will not be forthcoming. And third, the periods spent in apprenticeship training on the job must provide genuine training and skills development for the worker, in turn imposing costs on the firm that are offset (in part or full) by the wage subsidy.

Apprentice allowances in Malawi. The levy-financed Industrial Training Fund in Malawi, which focused mainly on the support of the apprenticeship scheme, is now being replaced by a broader-based scheme covering additional levels of training provision and a wider range of skills beyond apprentice trades (Franz, Maleta, and Mtambo 1998). Some three quarters of levy income were expended on the reimbursement of apprenticeship wages. Apprentice allowances were provided during the four-year apprenticeship period—both during the initial year of full-time institutional training (paid by the government) and, subsequently, during the three years of indentured training (paid by the firm and reimbursed by the fund). From the second year on, apprentices received a fixed monthly allowance, including the annual three-month period of block release at training institutions.

Combining the carrot with "ear-stroking"

All of the subsidy measures discussed above offer financial incentives to companies to increase their training efforts. But, as with the proverbial case of the stubborn mule, these carrots may not be attractive enough to influence behavior as much as desired. The British economist, the late Sir Dennis Robertson, once referred (in a different context) to the efficacy of "ear-stroking," whereby efforts at persuasion may be employed to complement the offer of incentives. A regime of financial incentives alone may be insufficiently strong to achieve the desired increase in enterprise training; the addition of more positive measures may be required. Indeed, financial incentives may prove to be a weak tool for generating more and better training, particularly over the long term, because they emphasize financial reward and not the value to the firm of the greater training investments themselves. Here then lies an important role for the state (or specialized agency) in promoting enterprise training through creating an informed climate of opinion conducive to company training. Measures would include dissemination of information on the benefits to the company of training, the provision of training advisory services, productivity consulting, training assistance, and know-how. Experience suggests that these activities are more likely to achieve success where provided by a central specialized training agency or training fund.

Lessons for policy

Many countries have policies that subsidize enterprise training, with the objective of enhancing the quantity and quality of company training provision. Three widely considered methods are direct public subsidies, training grants within the context of a levy-grant system, and company tax concessions. Company tax concessions have not been favored worldwide or in SSA. In this final section, we discuss some problems that are common to all three approaches. We then consider the major advantages and weaknesses of the alternative mechanisms (though on occasion, as in Mauritius, they are used in concert). Finally, some key points in policy design are recorded.

Mechanisms for encouraging enterprise training: strengths and limitations

Common weaknesses. The three mechanisms for encouraging enterprise training share a number of weaknesses. Table 9.1 lists these common weaknesses, provides a brief explanation of each, and offers some directions for improvement in policy. A central problem in designing policies to counter these weaknesses is that a policy measure may lead to an improvement in one weakness but exacerbate another. Thus, the redesign of training eligibility criteria to avoid training distortions may lead to higher inspection and monitoring costs, as will improved inspection methods to counter repackaging. A lightening of the administrative requirements on firms may well lead to an increase in company uptake of subsidies, but at the expense of data availability for inspection and monitoring. So, a careful balance of policy measures will be necessary.

Alternative mechanisms. While sharing some common weaknesses, the three mechanisms are not equally effective. In Table 9.2, we list some of the major weaknesses and, if any, notable advantages of each approach. A major advantage of levy-grant systems is that they do not draw on public

Table 9.1 Weaknesses Common to All Three Mechanisms

Weakness	Explanation	Policy directions
Windfalls	Eligible training may have been provided by the enterprise even in the absence of the incentive scheme	Revoke subsidy, if windfalls are widespread
Training distortions	May bias training towards more formal and externally-provided training, away from informal training on the job	Redesign training eligibility criteria to avoid distortions
Repackaging effect	"The adaptation and documentation of existing training provision to comply with eligibility requirements…" (Dougherty and Tan 1991)	Better inspection methods
High costs of inspection	The central costs of inspection and monitoring, to counter abuse by enterprises, may be high	Raise sanctions and monitor enterprises on a sample basis
Administrative costs on the firm	The cost to the enterprise of establishing eligibility and compliance (including paperwork and record-keeping) may be considerable	Avoid cumbersome administrative procedures/ onerous eligibility criteria

Table 9.2 Mechanisms for Encouraging Enterprise Training: Strengths and Weaknesses

Mechanism	Notable Advantages	Weaknesses
General training subsidies (grants)		Cost burden falls on public budgets (increased expenditures)
Levy-grant systems	Costs do not fall on public budgets—they are met by enterprises (or, with incidence shifting, by workers). Can facilitate a more systematic, structured approach to enterprise training.	
Company tax concessions		Requires a well-developed and broadly based system of corporate taxation. Cost burden of the scheme falls largely on public budgets (reduced revenues). Responsiveness of firms often low because few firms earn sufficient profits to benefit from the tax exemptions

funds, an important point in times of tight government budgets; in addition (as discussed above) they can lead to more systematic, structured enterprise training (though they often are not designed to do so). The disadvantages of tax-concession schemes militate against their adoption in other than a very few countries.

CHAPTER 10

Financing Informal Sector Training

The informal sector: a vehicle for employment growth

This paper has been largely silent on the question of the financing needs of the self-employed, small firms, and microenterprises, which we group together as the informal sector. Indeed, this reflects the existing balance of attention between informal and formal sector training in practice; the "training sector" is oriented toward the needs of formal sector employment. This is the case whether seen in terms of the type of course offerings in training institutions, the concerns and budget allocations of national training funds, or in the coverage and focus of levy-grant schemes.

Yet, this relative "neglect" of the informal sector is out of kilter with the realities of SSA labor markets. While in Latin America, urban formal employment has grown faster than that in the informal sector in the last two decades, in Southeast Asia the share of urban informal sector in nonagricultural employment is about 60 percent and growing. In Africa, the employment share of the informal sector is dominant (with a few notable exceptions such as South Africa and Zimbabwe); formal sector wage employment declined from 12 percent of the labor force in the 1980s to 9 percent in the 1990s (Gill, Dar, and Fluitman 1999). Typically, in SSA countries a growing labor force cannot be absorbed into formal sector employment since government employment growth is no longer feasible and opportunities for increased employment in the private formal sector are limited. Thus, in many countries in the region, substantial employment—and output—growth will be forthcoming in coming decades only in the informal sector.

The importance of the informal sector growth is in social, as well as economic, terms, since future improvements in the well-being of disadvantaged groups (such as female self-employed and rural populations) depend upon informal sector growth. Yet, skills development for this sector has not kept up with changing needs. Traditional apprenticeship, geared as it often is to transmitting existing practice, may still be appropriate in many settings; but it often results in low productivity and falls short of supplying the skills that technological development and industrial change require. In parallel, institutional training is aimed at a static formal sector and is not well tailored to the needs of informal sector employment and self-employment.

Developing informal sector training markets

There is now a voluminous literature on skills development for the informal sector that is critical of training within the informal sector (particularly the traditional apprenticeship) and describes the mixed record of new training initiatives aimed at, but often external to, the informal sector. A treatment of this material is beyond the scope of this chapter. Here we are concerned with the more limited issue of the financing aspects of these developments.

Departing from traditional training

Traditionally, training for the informal sector has been provided within the sector itself. Skill acquisition may take many forms, ranging from ad hoc, unsystematic learning on the job to more formal apprenticeships. But in all events the training is generally received within the context of the day-to-day production activities of the firm itself. The system was self-financing; trainees paid for training in the form of fees or low wages, and there was no financing role for government. In many contexts, informal sector training (as is the case for informal sector production) seemed to work well.

But, increasingly, these informal sector training markets have been too limited in meeting the broader skill needs associated with industrial development and growth. Apart from "learning by observing and doing," training is largely confined to initial training; continuing training and upgrading are rarely available. And the system is highly traditional in terms of skills and know-how imparted. There may be little scope for importing and teaching new methods, technologies, and entrepreneurial or management skills, all of which will be necessary to serve the growing entry flow into self-employment.

Introducing external training

The need to meet these shortcomings through appropriate training courses by *external* training providers is clear; these courses would complement internal skills acquisition. Public training institutions, financed through budgetary allocations, have not been suitable for this task, focused as they are on the needs of formal sector employment; hence, the need to build up a training supply response, in terms of specialized training providers geared toward the needs of the sector. We will subsequently discuss some of these efforts.

Demand for these training services may be weak, however, because information is not widely available and the desire to train may not be strong. And, of course, even if free, training is time-consuming, carrying opportunity costs; hence, these courses are usually heavily subsidized. While cost recovery is usually nominal at best, some county schemes have developed mechanisms (such as vouchers of entitlement) to raise effective demand (willingness to pay) for these services.

We now consider some SSA experiences in responding to the need for externally based training for the informal sector.

Funding informal sector training in SSA

Supply-side interventions

We note three highly subsidized, supply-side interventions (in Zimbabwe, Tanzania, and Madagascar), each operating within a different financing context, though in each case, these projects were funded from donor, rather than domestic, sources.

National training funds financed by a payroll levy system are in place in Zimbabwe and Tanzania (in the former case a levy-grant system, in the latter, revenue generation); but in neither case has the fund been centrally concerned, if at all, with the training needs of the informal sector or with its financing. In both cases this unfilled role has been taken up by donor agency initiatives in developing and financing separate training projects for the informal sector.

Zimbabwe has a large number of institutions that in various ways contribute toward the development of small enterprise and informal sector development; these are outlined in Kapoor, Mugwara, and Chidavaenzi (1997). Relatively little attention is given, however, to the training needs of the informal sector. A notable exception is the Traditional Apprenticeship Programme (TAP), a GTZ-financed pilot intervention (now in the replication stage), which aims at enhancing traditional practice in typical informal sector apprenticeships. It does so through providing the apprentice with initial short-term technical training and, where necessary, short-term follow-up training, which is complementary to the major component of apprenticeship training that is conducted in the workshop. Apprentices, as a prerequisite for entry to the program, must secure apprenticeship attachment; they attend formal courses against a participation fee. A central objective is to provide a route to sustained self-employment in the informal sector. Much emphasis is placed on building up a supply response from existing colleges and training centers; participation as a TAP training provider can be at a relatively low cost because the infrastructure and spare capacity of existing training institutions are used, particularly during evenings and vacation periods.

In Tanzania too, GTZ has developed pilot training programs for the informal sector, but in this case it has done so within the framework of and in cooperation with the Tanzanian training authority, VETA. These programs, however, represent a small part of VETA's present activities, though they may grow substantially in the future. The program, Integrated Training for Entrepreneurship Promotion (INTEP), aims at providing training opportunities for potential and existing micro and small enterprises (with special attention given to gender balance) in fields that VETA regional offices have found to offer good business prospects. The pilot training programs were predominantly donor funded, though some financial support was provided by the training levy and VETA facilities were used. As in many training initiatives for the informal sector, while the concept of cost sharing is integral to the INTEP program, in practice participants contributed only small amounts in fees.

Efforts in Madagascar to sponsor and develop training for the informal sector are also essentially donor agency funded. They are carried out, however, as a major part of the activities of the national training fund (financed mainly by donors, with about a 10 percent contribution from government). The National Council of Technical and Vocational Education, which manages the Intervention Fund for Vocational Training, changed its orientation in 1995 (seemingly at the behest of donors) from training support for the formal sector toward financing projects meeting the needs of small firms and the informal sector, in particular where growth potential was high.

Cross-subsidy—Côte d'Ivoire. The Vocational Training Development Fund (FDFP) in Côte d'Ivoire outsources training for the informal sector to specialized training providers to service target groups, including rural women. The program is of interest because training is financed from the proceeds of the training levy, from which small firms are exempt. Thus, the program cross-subsidizes informal sector training by using levy funds raised from formal sector employers. The cross-subsidy constitutes about a fifth of the fund's allocations for training. FDFP finances training projects submitted by "sponsors" (individuals, firms, or organizations) for defined target groups, including female entrepreneurs. Training is provided by preapproved training institutions (public or private) on the basis of competitive bids. Cost sharing at the outset was minimal; trainees paid no fees but absorbed any indirect costs such as transport. Since 1998, cost recovery has increased substantially, and trainees contribute 10 to 15 percent of costs through fee payment or contributions in kind.

Voucher schemes

Voucher schemes, operational in a number of SSA countries, aim at building up consumer demand for training courses for the informal sector and at facilitating a competitive response among training providers through consumer choice of institution and courses. As discussed in Chapter 8, voucher schemes typically do not lighten the financing burden falling on the funding body (usually the government); training remains subsidized, and cost recovery is not an integral part of the scheme (though it may be present). But vouchers can lead to greater cost-effectiveness of training provision, wider consumer (trainee) choice, and an improved demand orientation of training for the informal sector.

Subsidy schemes—Kenya and Ghana. The largely successful Kenyan scheme is perhaps the best known and most fully developed training voucher scheme operating in SSA. The flawed training voucher scheme planned, but never fully implemented, in Ghana shows some of the pitfalls in voucher scheme design.

Like the supply-side interventions discussed above, the Kenyan scheme is financed mainly by donor funding; it operates outside the framework of the Industrial Training Levy. The highly innovative Jua Kali (micro and small enterprise) voucher program, launched in 1996, is funded by the Micro and Small Enterprise Training Fund, and run by a privately managed Project Coordination Office (PCO) attached in the relevant ministry (in the past five years the PCO has been in five ministries). The scheme is directed toward established small business owners and employees, rather than new entrants, and operates on both the demand and supply side of the training market for informal sector skills. We provide little more than a synoptic account of the working of the scheme (Figure 10.1); a detailed description is provided in Riley and Steel (2000).

On the supply side, the scheme has goals similar to supply-side schemes discussed above. An important objective of the scheme is to widen the pool of training providers (including master craftsmen) that are capable of catering to the needs of the Jua Kali sector. In the initial stage, a pool of public and private training providers is preapproved, and selected on a competitive basis, in designated skill areas and competencies.

The novel elements of the scheme, however, are found on the demand side. Private allocation agencies are appointed, on the basis of competitive tender, to distribute (and market) training vouchers; the use of these intermediary bodies is a critical element of the scheme to ensure that vouchers are taken up and that advice and assistance is available to potential trainee applicants. The private allocation agencies include private consulting firms, NGOs, and Jua Kali associations. Allocation agents receive a fee equal to 3 percent of the value of vouchers issued. The allocation agent assists applicants in completing voucher applications (which also serve as a screening device to ensure that vouchers are issued to targeted recipients, defined in terms of equity and poverty alleviation). Following approval, the agent will issue the voucher to the applicant, on payment of the designated fee (at present 10 percent of the voucher value). Voucher recipients enroll in courses offered by preapproved training providers; upon course completion, the allocation agency presents the voucher to the PCO, which authorizes payment to the training provider.

An unplanned, though very positive, outcome was the emergence of a new kind of training provider that, although well placed to meet market needs for short, practical training, was largely unidentified: the skilled master craftsmen. Using vouchers to express their preferences with regard to training providers, Jua Kali workers assigned 85 percent of vouchers to buy the training services of master craftworkers, the remainder going to private and public training institutions.

Though sullied somewhat by implementation shortcomings, voucher payment delays, and even outright corruption, the demand-led voucher scheme is regarded as mainly successful. It is meeting the central objectives of building the elements of market demand for informal sector specific training and generating a supply-side response in the form of training providers able to meet the needs of informal sector businesses. Over the medium term, however, sustainability will require continued and substantial levels of subsidy as willingness to pay for training develops at a slow pace. As the market develops, cost sharing is planned to increase to 50 percent.

In Ghana, efforts to tackle supply- and demand-side issues within a joint framework were less successful. On the supply side, the development of training programs for the informal sector, with the active involvement of microenterprise trade associations, has continued apace. However, the use of "intake vouchers" for apprenticeship training was planned but never fully implemented.

The planned process comprised the annual distribution of intake vouchers by the National Vocational Council to trade associations, the number of vouchers issued being contingent on the availability of training places in each subject area. The associations would issue vouchers to their member master craftsmen, who in turn would allocate them to relevant workers. The apprentice would enroll at a local, preapproved private or public training institution, to which entry was restricted to voucher holders. The voucher scheme was unsuccessful and has been replaced by direct trainee recruitment by both trade associations and training institutions. It would appear that the vital intermediary role played by incentive-motivated private allocation agencies in the Kenyan scheme was sorely lacking here. Moreover, the lack of approved training providers in certain locations denied voucher holders the main benefit of a voucher scheme: consumer choice (and its consequent impact on efficiency, cost, and relevancy of training).

Financing through levy-grant—Mauritius. The voucher scheme in Mauritius is unusual in providing a framework within the levy-grant scheme whereby small and micro firms, all subject to the payroll levy, receive training benefits under the scheme. Undertraining has been endemic in small firms in Mauritius, the result of both an inadequate training culture

Figure 10.1. Voucher Scheme for Informal Sector Training

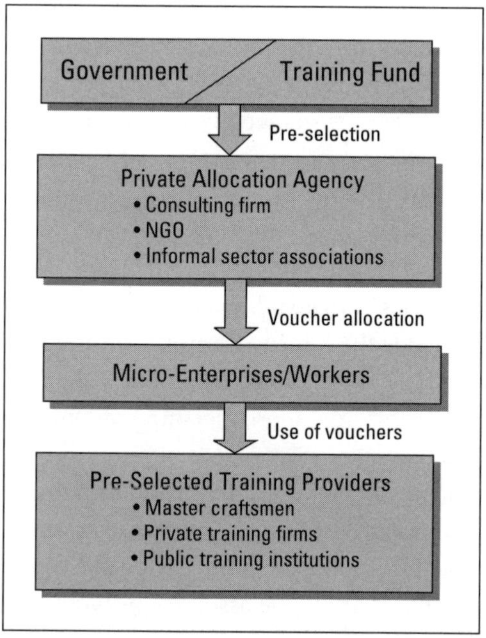

in such firms and the difficulties encountered by them in organizing training—something that the existing training incentives under the levy-grant scheme did little to overcome. Incorporated into the levy-grant arrangements in 1996, the voucher scheme allows for the provision of vouchers to small firms that may be used to pay (in part or fully) for training received from approved training providers meeting small firm needs. Vouchers are redeemed for payment from the Industrial and Vocational Training Board. The system would lead to an increase in interfirm equity of treatment under the levy-grant scheme, lighten the administrative burden that may weigh heavily on small firms in making reimbursement claims, and ease their cash-flow problems (Franz 2000).

Policy dilemmas in financing training for the informal sector

Throughout the SSA region, considerable population (and labor force) growth, combined with minimal increases in employment for the combined public and formal private sectors, will place a greater absorption burden on the informal sector. While traditional informal sector training markets, characterized by unstructured within-firm skills acquisition, have served the sector well in many locations and business environments (and frequently continue to do so), the system is too narrow to cope with the increasing challenges emanating from technical change, skills enhancement, and the widening of geographical markets. Public institutional training has not been able to adapt to the skill needs of the informal sector. Thus, an increasingly central role for specialized training providers (external to the firm) is now seen, for entry training into new skill areas and developing markets as well as for informal sector workers and proprietors. But private markets have been unable to fill this void; while there are numerous private market initiatives, they have been insufficient in quantity and skills.

Training markets have failed to develop because of market imperfections on the sides of both demand and supply. Effective demand (and a willingness to pay) for external training may be stunted for many reasons, including a lack of awareness of individual skill shortcomings and of information on economic opportunities for use of any newly acquired skills.

And there is a two-way information problem: on the one hand the lack of training supply means that potential trainees have little scope to develop knowledge about training opportunities, since these are potential only, and not available in the market. On the other hand, there is little incentive for new suppliers to emerge, given the lack of demonstrated demand and the risks involved in pioneering new training forms to meet the requirements of the sector.

This defines a central role for government (or training authority or donor) in developing these training markets. Most initiatives have been on the supply side, in the provision of courses leading to self-employment in newly developing markets (Tanzania and Madagascar). Others have been directed toward in-service skills acquisition (Côte d'Ivoire, Kenya, Zimbabwe). Some initiatives aim at generating effective demand for these training courses and increased cost sharing. In the case of the voucher scheme in Kenya an additional effect has been the identification (and supply response) of a novel form of training provision for the sector: courses by master craftsman within a familiar workshop setting. But generally, because effective demand for these courses is weak, they remain very heavily subsidized.

How may this substantial subsidy be justified? The case is strongest (on social grounds) for preentry courses that facilitate transfer into self-employment. These are frequently targeted at disadvantaged and poverty groups—rural women, for example—and we have argued that there is wide agreement on the legitimacy of a financing role for government here. Cost recovery can only be minimal in these cases. The case is less clear for in-service training, especially over the medium term. This training provides few of the wider externality benefits that might justify subsidy, and an ability (though not willingness) to pay is not clearly lacking. The case for subsidy is even less strong on benefit grounds for interfirm cross-subsidization, financed through levy payments by formal sector enterprises. However, a number of countries have moved in this direction (Côte d'Ivoire, South Africa). These considerations highlight the need to employ training subsidies as an interim learning tool, with increased cost sharing gradually replacing the subsidy. But most schemes have been able to move only slowly in this direction. The emergence of independent, self-sustained training markets for the informal sector remains a long way off.

CHAPTER 11

Financing Mechanisms: Contribution to Broad Policy Objectives

So far we have examined, within the SSA context, the use of funding mechanisms for financing training. The focus of this chapter is different. Ultimately, government establishes a financing framework in order to achieve a range of policy objectives in the training sphere. Financing mechanisms can contribute to reaching these policy objectives. In constructing a financing framework for the training system, government will recognize the role that financing mechanisms (which constitute part of the financing framework) can play in achieving policy objectives.

In Table 11.1 we outline the matching system between general policy objectives in the training sphere and between those measures (discussed at various points in the paper) that may be employed to achieve them. Drawn from the discussion in earlier chapters, the strengths and weaknesses of these mechanisms are recorded, and SSA country examples are noted. The table might serve as a checklist for policymakers and their advisers for available finance interventions that may be employed, alone or in concert with others.

Table 11.1 Policy Objectives and Financing Mechanisms, SSA

Policy Objective	Financing Mechanism	SSA Country Examples	Notable Strengths(S) / Weaknesses (W)
1. Raising additional or alternative funding for public sector training	Earmarked training taxes (usually based on company payroll)	Tanzania	Can provide a stable and protected source of funding for national training provision (S).
			Employers may shift the incidence of the levy on to workers in the form of lowered wages; then workers and not the employers bear the burden of the tax (W).
			Payroll levies may constitute an over-sheltered source of funding, leading to unspent surpluses, inefficiencies, and top-heavy bureaucracies (W).
			Employers may shift the incidence of the levy on to workers in the form of lowered wages; then workers and not the employers bear the burden of the tax (W). Payroll levies marginally raise the cost of labor to employers, possibly discouraging employment (W).
			Earmarked taxations do not conform well with the principles of sound public finance and weaken attempts to unify the national tax system (W). Under fiscal pressure, government may incorporate training levy proceeds into general public tax revenues (W).
			Levy proceeds may be diverted to non-training uses (W).
	Co-financing (matching funds)		Exerts pressure on training institutions to generate funding (S).
	Cost sharing (particularly trainee fees)	Kenya (Jua Kali project)	Trainees legitimately share in the cost burden of human capital creation, from which they are direct beneficiaries (S).
			The poor may be excluded from training opportunities unless targeted subsidies/ scholarships are available (W).

			Under fiscal pressure, government may incorporate training levy proceeds into general public tax revenues (W).
	Deferred trainee fees (government secured or subsidized loans)		Availability of trainee loans facilitates a policy of raising training fees and cost sharing (S). For most SSA countries where student loans are in place, the track record has been poor; loans for trainees will not fare better (W).
	Revenue generation by training providers:	Tanzania Botswana	Renting out facilities: fuller use of otherwise underutilized facilities (S).
	Production-for-profit/ training-with-production	Botswana	May lead to training outcomes more closely geared to the needs of the market (S). Neglect of the training function, lowering the quality and quantity of training (W). Too many resources may go to production activities rather than training (W). Income may not remain with the training institution (W).
	Promoting private training provision		Expansion of the national training system can be achieved without commitments of public funds (S). The concentration of private providers on low cost, high demand courses, may leave public sector institutions with the more costly, technical courses and limited possibilities for across-course subsidization (W).
	Donor aid (grants, loans)	Madagascar	Donor aid may be earmarked for training that is not appropriate for the country setting (W).
2. Promoting enterprise-based training (formal sector)	Fiscal incentives: company income tax concessions	Mauritius	Requires a well-developed and broadly based system of corporate taxation (W). Cost burden of the scheme falls largely on public budgets—reduced revenues (W).

(Continued)

Table 11.1 *(continued)*

Policy Objective	Financing Mechanism	SSA Country Examples	Notable Strengths(S) / Weaknesses (W)
			Responsiveness of firms often low because few firms earn sufficient profits to benefit from the tax exemptions (W).
			Firms may not respond to the tax incentive or may benefit from the subsidy without increased training efforts (W).
	Subsidies/grants from government or national training fund	Madagascar	Cost burden falls on public budgets—increased public expenditures (W).
			Firms may not respond to the incentive or may benefit from the subsidy without increased training efforts (W).
	Levy-grant systems: training cost reimbursement, training levy exemption, training cost redistribution	Côte d'Ivoire Mauritius Nigeria	May facilitate a more systematic, structured approach to enterprise training (S).
			Given their particular training needs, many firms, particularly small ones, do not benefit from the scheme; this breeds resentment, opposition and compromises the status of training levies as "benefit taxation" (W).
			Firms may not respond to the incentive or may benefit from the subsidy without increased training efforts (W).
	Industry training boards	Kenya Nigeria	May offer training promotion ,advisory and other services (S). May be ineffectual unless has genuine authority, autonomy and stakeholder representation (W).
	Training quotas	Not in SSA	May be too blunt a weapon to take account of differing training needs across firms and sectors (W).
			Firms may find it preferable to pay a fine for non-compliance rather than invest sufficiently in training provision to meets the quota (W).

	Promoting "modern" apprenticeships	South Africa (learnerships)	
	Legislation: training investment protection		
3. Improving efficiency and effectiveness of public training institutions	Output-based funding of training institutions		Introduces equitable and objective criteria for funding allocation (S). Promotes demand-driven training (S).
	Competitive bidding for funding, by training institutions	South Africa Côte d'Ivoire Senegal	Competition lowers public cost of training support (S). Bidding that is open to private as well as public training providers—strengthening the movement towards lower cost provision (S).
	Decentralization/ institutional autonomy	Madagascar Mauritius Tanzania—planned	Local institutional initiative better able to identify and meet local training needs (S). Local autonomy in budgetary allocations will facilitate development of locally appropriate, demand-driven training (S). If carried too far, central coordination of the training system may be placed in jeopardy (W). Local management of training institutions may be weak in the absence of appropriate staff development (W).
	Contract training		Secures required skills development for special target groups (S).
4. Effective allocation of national training resources	National training authorities		May be unsuccessful unless sufficiently well resourced, with access to required expertise (W). May be ineffectual unless has autonomy, genuine authority and stakeholder representation (W).

(Continued)

Table 11.1 *(continued)*

Policy Objective	Financing Mechanism	SSA Country Examples	Notable Strengths(S) / Weaknesses (W)
5. Moving towards flexible, market-responsive training provision	Promoting private training provision		The concentration of private providers on low-cost, high-demand courses may leave public sector institutions with the more costly, technical courses and limited possibilities for across-course subsidization (W).
	Outcomes funding of training institutions		Strong financial incentives to eschew supply-dominated institutional training (S).
	Contract training decentralization/ institutional autonomy	South Africa Kenya	Secures required skills development for special target groups (S). Local institutional initiative better able to identify and meet local training needs (S). Local autonomy in budgetary allocations will facilitate development of locally-appropriate, demand-driven training (S). If carried too far, central coordination of the training system may be placed in jeopardy (W). Local management of training institutions may be weak in the absence of appropriate staff development (W).
	Training vouchers/ accounts	Kenya	Promotes consumer/trainee choice (S). Can develop effective demand (willingness to pay) for training (S).
6 Equity objectives: training for minorities and special/ disadvantaged groups	Partnership: participation of stakeholders		Substantial representation of the major stakeholders on management board engenders a sense of ownership and cooperation in national resource management and facilitates (S).
	Normative financing for disadvantaged groups Targeted scholarships		

	Targeted vouchers		Promotes consumer/trainee choice (S). Can develop effective demand (willingness to pay) for training (S).
	Special allocations from Training Funds, particularly when financed by payroll levies	South Africa	Training levies collected from formal sector employers can serve as a vehicle for cross subsidization of training, from the formal sector to minority and special groups (S). May be opposed by formal sector firms, as weakening the benefit principle of training taxes (W).
7. Equity: training/retraining the unemployed	Contract training		Secures required skills development for special target groups (S).
8. Equity: meeting the needs of disadvantaged regions	Regionally targeted special allocations from Training Funds	Tanzania (not well implemented)	Regionally-based funding allocations may be self-serving if subject to political pressures from local vested interests (W).
	Regional training boards	Tanzania Madagascar	May be difficult to maintain a balance between central coordination and local autonomy (W).
9. Improving training for the informal sector and for self-employment	Training Funds	South Africa	Training levies collected from formal sector employers can serve as a vehicle for cross subsidization of training, from the formal to the informal sector (S).
	Vouchers	Kenya	Promotes consumer/trainee choice (S). Can develop effective demand (willingness to pay) for training (S).
10. Attracting foreign physical investment	Subsidized training for foreign companies which establish new, local production facilities	Not in SSA	

CHAPTER 12

Conclusions: Major Policy Messages

In Chapter 1, we outlined an emerging consensus about reforming the funding of training in developing countries. The major elements of this policy consensus, summarized in Table 12.1 (reproduced from Table 1.1) have constituted the underlying themes of this paper. It is within the framework of this policy consensus that we present the major policy messages emerging from this study.

There is now considerable agreement on what should be the main objective of training policy: *facilitating the development of effective, efficient, competitive, flexible, and responsive (demand-driven) training systems to meet national economic and social needs, and the needs of individuals.* Good training systems should reflect all five of these characteristics. We consider 15 finance-related issues that impinge on the goal of reaching this overall policy objective.

Redefined government role

In many SSA countries, government's role in both financing and providing training is excessive. While there is probably much more public *provision* of training than required by economic rationale, this may not be suboptimal if public training is efficient, effective, and market-responsive; unfortunately, this is often not the case. And it seems to be true that there is far more public *financing* of training than justified by the economic arguments adduced in Chapter 3. Constrained national budgets have exerted their toll on the quality and effectiveness of public training provision. These increasing pressures on government budgets provide an opening for the diversification funding for training—a major theme of this paper.

The appropriate role of government in training markets cannot be determined without referring to the capabilities of private training markets. Where they can function well they can be seen as an alternative to public sector provision; where they do not, then the public sector should be engaged. This approach to the appropriate role of government in training finance and provision requires that a country determines its individual needs for public sector training intervention. It will need to examine the performance of its markets, the capacity of the private sector to deliver training, and its own preferences about social policies and equity. On this basis, in most countries the state is likely to retain a central and continuing role in the delivery and, particularly, in the financing of training.

Funding diversification

In national training systems where public training budgets are constrained, mechanisms for augmenting resources available for training programs are usually developed. These entail a combination of measures such as reduced training subsidization and increased sharing of the training finance burden by other beneficiaries of the training system, particularly trainees and enterprises. This process is called funding diversification. Funding diversification can take many different forms. Chapter 7 outlines four different avenues that may be pursued, separately or in combination. Three act directly in bringing in additional revenues to the training sector while the fourth affects training budgets only indirectly. Thus, additions to total funding available for allocation to training providers may be secured through the levying of payroll taxes. Again, training institutions may augment public budgetary allocations through cost sharing (in particular, through introducing or raising course fees) and through income generation (largely from combining production with training). And, finally, encouragement may be given to the development of private training institutions.

Table 12.1 Training Finance: The Emerging Policy Consensus

Overall training policy objective: To facilitate the development of effective, efficient, competitive, flexible and responsive (demand-driven) Training markets, to meet national economic and social needs and the needs of individuals	
Role of training finance in moving towards this objective	Explanation
1. Redefined government role	Redefinition of government role (diminished, but still critical), entailing reduced public budgetary support for formal sector institutional training
2. Funding diversification	Diminished government financing role is to be accompanied by a diversification of sources of financing, greater cost recovery and cost sharing
3. Cost sharing	Moves towards increased cost sharing, with higher, more realistic training fees (with scholarships for the needy) and perhaps state-backed student/trainee loans
4. Training levies	Funding diversification measures to include training levies on enterprises
5. Income generation	Funding diversification measures also include income generation by public training institutions
6. Decentralization	Income generation objectives would be furthered through decentralization of control over public sector providers and greater institutional autonomy
7. Private sector	Government to encourage private sector provision of training
8. Funding public training institutions	Replace arbitrary, ad hoc funding arrangements by objective formula funding related to inputs, outputs and outcomes. Consider case for subsidy of selected private training institutions
9. Trainee/consumer choice	More voice is to be accorded to trainee/consumer choice; vouchers may help develop the demand side of the market where subsidy needs to be retained
10. Levy-grant	Levy-grant mechanisms to be introduced where formal sector enterprises under-train
11. Training funds	National training funds to be developed, to take a broader and longer term view of training expenditures in a national context
12. Training authorities	Where institutionally possible, fully-fledged, autonomous national training authorities to be established
13. Stakeholders	Increased participation of stakeholders (especially employers) in national training policy formation and execution
14. Disadvantaged groups	Continuing and enhanced government role in skills development as an integral part of a package of measures to assist disadvantaged groups
15. Informal sector	Central attention to be paid to largely neglected training needs of small micro enterprises and informal sector producers

These diversification options are not alternatives; all four avenues may be explored simultaneously. Whether to do so, however, and to what extent, remains a policy issue that must be settled within the context of conditions ruling in each country.

Training fees

Many countries are moving toward increased cost sharing, with the imposition of higher, more realistic training fees, scholarships for the needy, and perhaps state-backed student/trainee loans. There is little conformity of practice in tuition fees policy across countries. The feasibility of tuition fee setting (in relation to unit costs of training) is a compound of many and diverse factors, which will vary from place to place. They include (a) type and costs of training, (b) the price elasticity of trainee demand for different training courses, (c) political constraints, and (d) policies for equality of opportunity. Thus, it is not possible to be prescriptive in regard to the scope for generating revenues from tuition fees; this will need to be settled on a case-by-case basis, in light of local conditions and possibilities.

A central issue in fee policy is whether a regime of standard, national compulsory fees should be instituted or whether individual training institutions should be given the freedom to fix the level of fees overall, differing by the type of training course. Institutional autonomy in the setting of fees, while representing a more desirable approach, may not be feasible in otherwise centralized training systems. But while standard, compulsory fee setting may be an inflexible tool, unlikely to reflect local market realities, it is generally acceptable as a second-best measure.

The positive financial benefits from greater cost recovery need to be examined alongside the potentially adverse effects on equity. There is a clear tradeoff here. Higher, realistic fees will exclude from training those who are unable to pay; fees set at comfortably low levels will not make a sizable contribution to cost recovery. In particular, negative impacts on the access to training opportunities of the poor, minorities, rural populations, and other disadvantaged groups are likely. This shows the widely recognized need to introduce targeted subsidies directed to these at-risk groups, in the form of scholarships and reduced fees. Targeting those most in need within these groups, however, particularly in the SSA context, has not been easy.

Cost sharing through user fees will discourage participation in formal training programs, even by the nonpoor. The classic solution to this problem, encountered most often in higher education, is deferred cost recovery in the form of student loans. But the record for student loan schemes in SSA countries is poor. The sound administration of a loans scheme requires appropriate, high-level, institutional support—which is rare in many SSA countries. Given the lack of success in administering student loan schemes in SSA, it is unlikely that training loans would fare better.

Training levies

In many countries, particularly in Latin America, the dominant tool for funding augmentation is the training levy, usually levied as a percentage of payroll. Levy proceeds are used mainly to support public sector training provision, with the emphasis on initial training at formal public training institutions.

In the SSA context especially, payroll levy schemes of this type (though not widely adopted) may be a valuable mechanism for greater funding diversification, lightening the burden of training funding falling on the state. The expectation is that levy income would complement existing government financing, thus providing an additional source of funding; however, this has not always been the case in practice. In addition to generating more funding for training, levies of this type can offer a more stable form of funding than do government allocations. However, training levies have worked well only in some SSA countries. Thus, particular attention will need to be accorded to levy scheme design in order to avoid some of the weaknesses that have been evident in the SSA context. These include poor levy collection outcomes, leakage of levy proceeds into general government revenues, and inequitable coverage (in terms of firm size and sectors to be included).

The scope for levying payroll taxes is well established by international experience in SSA countries and elsewhere: Almost all countries that have introduced payroll levies have set the levy rate in the range of 1 to 2 percent of company payroll bills, the majority at the lower end of the range.

Institutional income generation

Income generated from the sale of production and service activities of trainees can be a useful form of additional institutional income. Income may be derived as a by-product of the training process itself. But it is possible to utilize available skills and facilities to produce output for sale in the local market; indeed, exposure to local markets may bring about relevant, market-oriented training. Here the issue is one of maintaining a healthy balance between these two activities. As more weight is given to instruction, the income potential from production declines; alternatively, quality of training will suffer as emphasis is placed on production rather than instruction.

The proportion of recurrent expenses covered by production sales will vary considerably from case to case; the scope for generating income from production will depend on numerous local factors, including the nature of the product, local demand conditions, and potential market competition. If an acceptable balance is maintained between training quality and production for sale, the scope for cost recovery may be limited, usually accounting for only a small percentage of recurrent expenditure. In some exceptional cases, however, it can contribute a considerable proportion of total costs.

Training institutions may also generate income from the sale of services, including (a) renting out underused facilities and (b) providing consulting services to local enterprises.

As with training fee policy, local institutional initiative in income generation from production will be stunted if this income does not contribute to institutional budgets. This is the case where the sums collected are deducted from institutional budgetary allocations, and thus accrue to government budgets or the national training fund, and not to the training institution.

Decentralization

Institutional fee charging and income generation objectives can be advanced by decentralizing control over public sector providers and offering greater institutional autonomy. Where user fees are voluntary and left to local institutional initiative, it may encourage training providers to develop a more dynamic, even aggressive, approach to exploiting the potential of the local market environment. Institutional fee policy then becomes more than a device for cost recovery and cost sharing. In providing a mechanism for varying fee levels across courses and client groups, it serves as a tool for moving the training system toward open, demand-oriented training. In many cases, this condition is unmet. More often, it is recognized that fee policy and income generation are not set in a vacuum. Institutional-level fee fixing is usually but one element (ideally a central one) of more general, decentralized training systems with local institutional autonomy. It is only in this liberal context that the full potential of cost sharing and income generation is likely to be forthcoming.

Private sector development

The growth of private training institutions, with trainees paying full costs, offers a pathway for expanding the national training system without heavy commitments of public funds. Indeed, *reduced* public training provision could be possible (and concomitant budgetary reductions) with the reduction in public training supply made up by compensating expansion of private training institutions.

In many countries, the lack of private training provision results from financial, institutional, and other constraints that hold back private provider development. The imposition of restrictions such as legal prohibitions, tight regulatory control, and tuition fee ceilings may combine to render private institutional start-up problematic. While these restrictions are intended to protect the interests of potential trainees, they are often counterproductive in constraining private training supply. Governments can help establish a more liberal regulation regime, particularly aimed at quality control, combined with an enabling environment that encourages incipient private training institutions and dissemination of information about the quality of training institutions and courses, and their relevance to employment opportunities.

Funding public training institutions

An important task of funding disbursement policies, as discussed in Chapter 8, is to provide an appropriate mix of regulation and incentives to ensure public training can hold its own in an environment of competitive training markets. A much needed reform is the gradual dismantling of the arbitrary, ad hoc institutional core funding arrangements in place in almost all SSA countries, and their gradual replacement by objective funding formula, such as those related to inputs, outputs, and outcomes.

Trainee/consumer choice

In moving away from supply-dominated training markets, there should be more emphasis on developing trainee/consumer choice. The demand side of training markets—in which the consumer (trainee) will have a more central role—will be helped by increasing cost recovery at public training institutions through higher tuition fees, and by developing private training provision. Trainee choice, however, needs to be an informed choice. But relevant information on training opportunities and the relative advantages of various course offerings and institutions is often lacking, as is information on the relevance of courses to labor market demands; government has a clear role here in providing potential trainees with this information.

Where training subsidy needs to be retained, vouchers of entitlement to training courses may help to develop the demand side of the market; however, while training vouchers are rare in SSA countries, some training systems have initiated (limited and largely experimental) voucher schemes; their progress will be monitored with interest.

Levy-grant systems

Where formal sector enterprises undertrain, there may be a strong case for encouraging enterprise training through training incentives; and a particular case can be made for subsidized apprenticeship wages on grounds of equity and efficiency. Levy-grant systems (where the training grant to the enterprise is financed by a training levy) have some clear advantages over alternative incentive systems—notably direct government subsidy payments and concessions on enterprise tax obligations of companies that train. However, all three mechanisms share a number of weaknesses. As discussed in Chapter 9, these include the receipt of unnecessary windfalls, the encouragement of training distortions, repackaging, high inspection costs, and heavy administrative burden on the firm. A central problem in training grant design is to minimize the effects of these weaknesses.

A major advantage of levy-grant systems is that they do not draw on public funds, an important point in times of tight government budgets. In addition, they can lead to more systematic, structured enterprise training (though often they are not designed to do so). However, they may result in between-firm inequities if there is no close relationship between the burden of the levy and the benefits received.

The disadvantages of tax-concession schemes have militated against their adoption in other than a few countries.

Training funds

A national training fund may be seen as a unique institutional framework for unifying and augmenting public sources of funding for training and for allocating funds in line with national policies and priorities. While in older, established training funds, training levies were the dominant (usually only) income source, newer funds draw from a variety of available income sources, including government budgetary allocations, donor funding, and income generated by the fund itself. Indeed, in some cases training funds derive no income from training levies; either levies have not been instituted or, where in place, levy proceeds are regarded as general tax revenues and are not passed on to the fund.

With the broadening of income sources of training funds, training funds are now regarded as a general funding pool, distributed across various recipient destinations according to established priorities and policies. This often results in a great deal of cross-subsidization of training (especially of informal sector training from formal sector levy proceeds). Successful fund management seems to require autonomy of the management board in decisionmaking and its control over budget allocations; also, substantial representation of the major stakeholders on the management board (especially employers), engendering a sense of ownership, appears to be an additional ingredient of success.

An important objective of establishing national training funds (particularly when financed by company training levies) is to provide sustained and stable funding for the training programs they support. In practice this has not always been achieved, notably when funds do not receive the resources designated to finance its activities; training levy proceeds, designated for the training fund, may be absorbed instead into general government revenues. Training fund sustainability over the long term is a serious problem in some countries, in particular where training funds have been launched by donors and are funded, in the main, externally. This problem of fund sustainability will be endemic in those many SSA country situations where public budgets are severely constrained over the medium term, and where the time is not ripe for introducing training levies. In this situation, overgenerous external support for national training funds, without the planned, complementary development of domestic funding, will result in moribund training authorities and empty coffers.

Training authorities

Where institutionally possible, full-fledged, autonomous national training authorities should be established and given responsibility for national skills development. To respond to the developing skill needs of the economy, and to be in a position to be proactive in relation to ongoing technological and industrial change, public training systems need a greater degree of independence from line ministries. National training authorities will often play a central coordinating role in planning the national training system, in developing training policy, supervising national skills testing and certification, as well as in providing information services and developing labor market signals.

Stakeholder role

Participation of the main stakeholders (especially employers) in national training policy formation and management (such as through active membership of the governance institutions of training funds or national training authorities) has an important role to play in building consensus on training issues; this may be especially important where enterprise training levies are in place.

Needs of disadvantaged groups

A continuing and enhanced government role in skills development should form an integral part of a package of measures to assist disadvantaged groups. There is an increasing social awareness (and conscience) concerning the low status and skill needs of special groups, such as the poor, ethnic minorities, and women. In parallel, there is wide acceptance of the view that the government has an obligation to assist in this field, through financing and perhaps provision of special programs, aimed particularly at securing entry into the informal sector. These developments are likely to be heavily constrained by a lack of available government funding because they coincide with increasingly limited public budgets and greater intersectoral competition for funding allocations. This may indicate an appropriate role for donor intervention.

Informal sector training

The training needs of small microenterprises and informal sector producers must be addressed. Throughout SSA countries, considerable population (and labor force) growth, combined with minimal employment increases in the combined public and formal private sectors, place an increasing absorption burden on the informal sector. Traditional informal sector training markets, characterized by unstructured, within-firm skills acquisition, have served the sector well. The system is too narrow, however, to cope with the increasing challenges emanating from technical change, the need for skills enhancement, and the widening of geographical markets. Public institutional training has not been able to adapt to the skills needs of the informal sector. Thus, an increasingly central role for specialized training providers (external to the firm) is now seen, both for entry training into new skill areas and developing markets, as well as for informal sector workers and proprietors. Private markets have not been able to fill this void, thus defining a critical role for government initiatives, perhaps buttressed by donor support.

References

The word *processed* describes informally reproduced works that may not be commonly available through libraries.

Albrecht, Douglas, and Adrian Ziderman. 1991. "Deferred Cost Recovery for Higher Education: Student Loan Programs in Developing Countries." Discussion Paper No. 137. Washington, D.C.: The World Bank.

Atchoarena, David, ed. 1996. *The Financing and Management of Vocational Education and Training in Eastern and Southern Africa*. Paris: UNESCO/IEEP.

Athumani, A., and E. N. Ngowi. 1999. *Vocational Education and Training in Tanzania: The Reform Experiences 1990–1999*. Dar-es-Salaam.

Becker, Gary S. 1964. *Human Capital*. New York: National Bureau of Economic Research.

Bennell, Paul. 1993. "The Cost-Effectiveness of Alternative Training Modes in Zimbabwe." *Comparative Education Review* Vol. 37, No. 4.

—. 1996. "Privatization, Choice and Competition: The World Bank's Reform Agenda for Vocational Education and Training in Sub-Saharan Africa." *Journal of International Development* Vol. 8, No. 3.

Bolina, Pradeep. 1994. "Financing Vocational Education and Training in Developing Countries." In *Problems in Financing Vocational Education and Training in Developing Countries*. Mannheim: Zentralstelle fur Gewerbliche Berufsforderung (ZGB).

Bredie, Joseph. 1997. "Note on Provision and Financing of Training: Focus on IVTB." Processed.

CINTERFOR/ILO. 1990. *Vocational Training on the Threshold of the 1990s: A Study of Changes and Innovations in Specialized Institutions of Latin America*.

PHREE Background Paper Series No. 91/35. Vols. 1 and 2. Washington, D.C.: The World Bank.

Dar, Amit, Indermit Gill, and Joseph Bredie. 1997. "Proposal to Improve the Effectiveness and Efficiency of the Levy-Grant System—Republic of Mauritius." Washington, D.C.: The World Bank.

Dougherty, Christopher, and Jee-Peng Tan. 1991. *Financing Training: Issues and Options*. Population and Human Resources Department Working Paper Series No. 716. Washington, D.C.: The World Bank.

—. 1997. "Financing Training: Issues and Options." *International Journal of Manpower* Vol. 18, No. 1/2.

Drake, Keith. 1991. "Interventions in Market Financing of Training in the European Community." In Paul Ryan, ed., *International Comparisons of Vocational Education and Training for Intermediate Skills*. London: The Falmer Press.

Drake, Keith, and Jean-Francois Germe. 1994. *Financing Continuing Training: What are the Lessons from International Comparisons?* Thessaloniki, Greece: CEDFEFOP—European Centre for the Development of Vocational Training (December).

Ducci, Marie A. 1991. "Financing of Vocational Training in Latin America." Training Discussion Paper No. 71. Geneva: International Labour Office.

—. 1997. "New Challenges to Vocational Training Authorities: Lessons from the Latin American Experience." *International Journal of Manpower* Vol.18, No. 1/2.

Felstead, Alan. 1998. *Output-related Funding in Vocational Education and Training: A Discussion Paper and Case Studies*. Thessaloniki, Greece: CEDFEFOP—European Centre for the Development of Vocational Training.

Ferej, Ahmed. 1997. "The Kenya Training Fund." In World Bank: *Proceedings from the International Conference on Employment and Training Funds, Antalya, Turkey, 1997*. Economic Development Institute. Washington, D.C.: The World Bank.

Franz, Jutta. 2000. "Financing Training: Evidence from Other Countries." Handout prepared for the first Workshop on Developing a TVET Strategy for the Tigray National Regional State, Addis Ababa, June. Processed.

Franz, Jutta, Marc Maleta, and Maston Mtambo. 1998. "A New Mechanism for Financing TEVET in Malawi." A study commissioned by the TEVET Secretariat. Processed.

Gasskov, Vladimir, ed. 1994. *Alternative Schemes of Financing Training*. Geneva: International Labour Office.

Gill, I., A. Dar, and F. Fluitman. 1999. "Constraints and Innovation in Reforming National Training Systems: Cross-Country Comparisons." *International Journal of Manpower* Vol. 20, No. 7.

—. 2000. *Skills and Change: Constraints and Innovations in the Reform of Vocational Education and Training.* New York: Oxford University Press.

Haan, Hans C. 2001. *Training for Work in the Informal Sector: Fresh Evidence from Sub-Sahara Africa.* Turin: ILO Training Centre.

Hegelheimer, Armin. 1988. *Financing of Vocational Training.* Mannheim: German Foundation for Economic Development (DSE).

Herschbach, Dennis. 1990. "Organizational Characteristics of National Training Agencies.. Draft version, April 9, 1990. Processed.

—. 1993. "Financing Vocational Training in Developing Countries." Training Discussion Paper No. 111. Geneva: International Labour Office.

—. 1994. "Financing Vocational Education and Training in Developing Countries." Training Discussion Paper No. 111. Geneva: International Labour Office.

ILO (International Labour Office). 1972. *Employment, Incomes and Equality. A Strategy for Increasing Productive Employment in Kenya.* Geneva.

Jager, Matthias, and Tobias Buhrer. 2000. "Financing TVET." Zurich: KODIS Consult GmbH. Processed Cooperation (SDC).

Johanson, Richard. 1995. *Diversifying Sources of Vocational Training Finance: A Set of Training Modules.* Training Policy and Programme Development Branch. Geneva: International Labour Office. Processed.

—. 2001. *Review of World Bank Projects in Technical-Vocational Education and Training (TVET) in Sub-Sahara Africa, 1990–2000—Case Study No. 1: Côte d'Ivoire.* Washington, D.C.: The World Bank. Processed.

Kapoor, Kapil, Doris Mugwara, and Isaac Chidavaenzi. 1997. *Empowering Small Enterprises in Zimbabwe.* Discussion Paper No. 379. Washington D.C.: The World Bank.

Katz, Eliakim, and Adrian Ziderman. 1990. "Investment in General Training: The Role of Information and Mobility." *Economic Journal* Vol. 100, December.

—. 1999. "A Government Role in Training Markets in Developing Countries: Theory and Policy." In Sami Daniel, Philip Arestas, and John Grahl, eds., *Regulation Strategies and Economic Policies.* Cheltenham, UK: Edgar Elgar.

Keep, Ewart. 1991. "The Grass Looked Greener—Some Thoughts on the Influence of Comparative Vocational Training Research on the UK Policy Debate." In Paul Ryan, ed., *International Comparisons of Vocational Education and Training for Intermediate Skills.* London: The Falmer Press.

King, Kenneth. 2001. "Enterprise-based Training in the Formal Sector of the Kenyan Economy: The New Dynamics." Second draft. Processed

Lauglo, Jon. 1992. "Vocational Training and the Bankers' Faith in the Private Sector." *Comparative Education Review* Vol. 36, No. 2.

Middleton, John, Adrian Ziderman, and Arvil V. Adams. 1993. *Skills for Productivity: Vocational Education and Training in Developing Countries.* New York: Oxford University Press.

Ministry of Science, Technology and Vocational Training, Zambia. 1997. *Strategy Paper for Technical Education, Vocational and Entrepreneurship Training (TEVET) in Zambia.*

National Training Board. 1986. *Implementation of a Cash Grant System of Tax Concession.* Pretoria: Department of Manpower.

Ndoro, Choice, and Lewis Durango. 2001. Utility of the Zimbabwe Manpower Development Fund (ZIMDEF). Report prepared on behalf of the Confederation of Zimbabwe Industries. Processed.

Noble, Charles. 1997. "International Comparisons of Training Policies." *Human Resource Management Journal* Vol. 7, No. 1.

Republic of South Africa. 1995. Government Notices: Department of Labour, No. R. 60. *Government Gazette, No. 16222.* Pretoria (January).

Riley, Thyra, and William Steel. 2000. "Kenya Voucher Program for Training and Business Development Services." In Jacob Levitsky, ed., *Business Development Services: A Review of International Experience.* London: Intermediate Technology Publications.

Ryan, Paul. 1991. "Introduction: Comparative Research on Vocational Education and Training." In Paul Ryan, ed., *International Comparisons of Vocational Education and Training for Intermediate Skills.* London: The Falmer Press.

Ssebuyoya, Z. G. 1997. *Report on the Implementation of Component II of the SAP (Strategic Action Plan).* Dar-es-Salaam.

Suhr, Katja. 2000. *Review of the Formal and Informal Apprenticeship Schemes in Zimbabwe.* Study commissioned by the Ministry of Higher Education and Technology. Harare: GTZ. Processed.

Tsang, Mun. 1997. "The Cost of Vocational Training." *International Journal of Manpower* Vol. 18, Nos. 1/2.

VETA (Vocational Education and Training Authority). 2000. *Establishment of Levy Collection Mechanism by VETA.* Report from the Finance-and-Tender Committee. Dar-es-Salaam. Processed.

Wallenborn, Manfred. 1994. "The Funding of Vocational Education and Training." In *Problems in Financing Vocational Education and Training in Developing Countries.* Mannheim: Zentralstelle fur Gewerbliche Berufsforderung (ZGB).

Wander, Hilde. 1987. "Population, Labor Supply and Employment in Developing Countries." *Annals of the American Academy of Political and Social Sciences.* No. 492. July.

Whalley, John, and Adrian Ziderman. 1990. "Financing Training in Developing Countries: The Role of Payroll Taxes." *Economics of Education Review* Vol. 9, No. 4.

World Bank. 1991. *Vocational and Technical Education and Training: A World Bank Policy Paper.* Washington, D.C.: The World Bank.

—-. 1997. *Proceedings from the International Conference on Employment and Training Funds, Antalya, Turkey, 1997.* Economic Development Institute. Washington, D.C.: The World Bank.

Ziderman, Adrian. 1978. *Manpower Training: Theory and Policy.* London: Macmillan.

—-. 1989. "Training Alternatives for Youth: Results for Longitudinal Data." *Comparative Education Review* Vol. 33, No. 2.

—-. 1990. "Financing Skills for Development: An Evolving Role for the Public Sector." In *Technical and Vocational Education and Training: Proceedings of the Regional Seminar on Technical and Vocational Education and Training.* Manila: Asian Development Bank.

Ziderman, Adrian, and Douglas Albrecht. 1995. *Financing Universities in Developing Countries.* The Stanford Series on Education and Public Policy. London: The Falmer Press.